TONGLEN

the path of transformation

tonglen
TONGLEN

the path of transformation

PEMA CHÖDRÖN

Edited by Tingdzin Ötro

Kalapa Publications • Halifax

Kalapa Publications
2178 Gottingen Street
Halifax, Nova Scotia
CANADA B3K 3B4
(902) 421.1550
kalapamedia.org

ISBN: 978-1-55055-002-3
10 9 8 7 6

Text designed by Merv Henwood

PRINTED IN CANADA

May all sentient beings enjoy happiness and the root of happiness.

May they be free from suffering and the root of suffering.

May they not be separated from the great happiness devoid of suffering.

May they dwell in the great equanimity free from passion, aggression, and prejudice.

CONTENTS

ACKNOWLEDGEMENTS

I would like to thank Lynne van de Bunte, who helped me obtain tapes of Pema's seminars, and the people who helped me transcribe the talks: Gigi Sims, Diana Church, and Michael Mikowski. I would also like to thank the staff at Vajradhatu Publications—Cheryl Campbell, Judith Lief, and Ellen Kearney—for their support and encouragement.

I would especially like to thank Pema for the opportunity to work with her over the past several years. She has been my friend, my mentor, and my colleague. What makes her a continuing inspiration is that she never gives up working on herself. In other words, she walks it like she talks it. Thanks, Pema.

Finally, I would like to dedicate my efforts on this book to my mother, Margaret Beard, who is a devout Christian. She gave me the gifts of life, of love, and of longing for spiritual truth.

May all beings be happy and at their ease! May they come to rest in their own basic goodness!

Tingdzin Ötro
(Scott Beard)
July 2000

For several years, Pema Chödrön has been teaching lojong seminars and giving instructions on the practice of tonglen in North America and Europe. At one time, tonglen was a relatively restricted practice within the Shambhala International community. Only people who had formally taken the bodhisattva vow were allowed to practice it. Now, in large part due to Pema's teaching, it has become much more widespread.

Sometimes people receive their first tonglen instruction during a weekend program and then find themselves basically on their own. Although they are inspired by the teachings, they may very well have a difficult time practicing at home. They may become discouraged, and perhaps give up altogether. This book was designed to help such new students, as well as older practitioners who want to deepen their current understanding. It will also be a useful reference for meditation instructors.

The book is primarily practice oriented, since Pema has already discussed the view of cultivating bodhichitta, and the philosophy behind it, in other books. People who would like to explore the view further could read *Start Where You Are* (especially Chapters One to Six) and *The Places That Scare You* (Shambhala Publications, 2001). For newer students, the first occurrence of terms that might be unfamiliar are printed in *italics* and are described in the glossary.

It is assumed that people who read this book are already familiar with the practice of sitting meditation, which is absolutely essential for properly entering into the practice of tonglen. If not, the basic technique is presented in all of Pema's other books, although it is best to learn it personally from a meditation instructor.

Tonglen was originally a Buddhist practice. But because it is a practice for getting in touch with the essence of our humanity—loving-kindness and compassion—I think that anyone can benefit from it. It can be used by followers of any religious tradition, as well as by those who choose not to follow a religious path.

TONGLEN

the path of transformation

The everyday practice is simply to develop a complete acceptance and openness to all situations and emotions, and to all people, experiencing everything totally without mental reservations and blockages, so that one never withdraws or centralizes onto oneself.

CHÖGYAM TRUNGPA RINPOCHE

All sentient beings without exception have *bodhichitta*, which is the inherent tenderness of the heart, its natural tendency to love and care for others. But over time, in order to shield ourselves from feeling pain and discomfort, we have erected solid barriers that cover up our tenderness and vulnerability. As a result, we often experience alienation, anger, aggression, and a loss of meaning in our lives—both individually and on a global scale. Somehow, in the pursuit of happiness, we have unwittingly created greater suffering for ourselves.

Tonglen, or the practice of sending and taking,

reverses this process of hardening and shutting down by cultivating love and compassion. In tonglen practice, instead of running from pain and discomfort, we acknowledge them and own them fully. Instead of dwelling on our own problems, we put ourselves in other people's shoes and appreciate our shared humanity. Then the barriers start to dissolve, our hearts and minds begin to open.

Before presenting the formal practice of tonglen, I would like to discuss a few ways that you can begin to incorporate the tonglen outlook into your daily life. After all, how you lead your life—with *maitri* and compassion for both yourself and others—is really the point. What's more, if you train in the outlook on a daily basis, you will find that the formal practice comes much more naturally.

Trungpa Rinpoche used to tell his students to live their lives as an experiment. In other words, be inquisitive, be open and without expectations, then see what happens and learn from your experience. For this reason, I often suggest that students chose a limited amount of time—say, three months or a year—to work with the tonglen approach, just to see how it affects their lives. But don't think that you will be able to perfect the practice in such a short time. Tonglen is really a practice for the rest of your life.

SITTING MEDITATION

Practicing sitting meditation, or *shamatha-vipashyana*, a little bit every day is a good way to start training in the tonglen attitude. It's a way of checking in with your state of mind, like holding up a mirror to yourself. Sitting cultivates both *absolute* and *relative* bodhichitta. As an absolute bodhichitta practice, it teaches us not to grasp at thoughts and emotions as solid. As a relative bodhichitta practice, it teaches us maitri and compassion for ourselves.

In general, it's not a good idea to start doing the formal tonglen practice until you have a good grounding in sitting meditation. You especially need to cultivate steadfastness, the courage and patience to sit with whatever arises during meditation. Otherwise, you might be knocked off your cushion by the emotions that tonglen provokes.

For that reason, it is always suggested that you begin and end with sitting meditation whenever you do tonglen.

Even if you're not on a cushion or in the meditation hall, you can experiment with the practice of mindfulness and awareness. You can use it as a tool to get in touch with what you are feeling in the present moment. For example, sometimes when I am alone or find myself in a quiet setting—taking a walk in the woods, gazing out my cabin window, or sitting on a bench by the ocean—I let go of my thoughts and try to see what lies underneath them.

Actually, this is the essence of mindfulness practice: always coming back to the immediacy of your present experience and letting go of thoughts and judgements about it. You will probably discover there is something that remains after you drop the thoughts and the story lines. What's left is the immediacy of the sense perceptions—sight, smell, touch, and so on—as well as a feeling or mood.

For example, perhaps the feeling underneath your thoughts is self-hatred. Consequently, when thoughts begin to bubble up, they sound like "bad, bad; good, good; should, shouldn't." When you become aware of such thoughts, you just let them go and come back to the immediacy of your experience. This in itself is the practice of maitri, or making friends with yourself.

MAKING ASPIRATIONS

I am a big fan of making aspirations. I think they are very helpful on our path, because they help us to stay in touch with our motivation to develop bodhichitta. The *lojong slogan*, "Two activities: one at the beginning, one at the end," suggests beginning and ending each day by reaffirming your motivation to dissolve barriers, to open your heart, and to reach out to people. When you wake up in the morning and go to bed at night, you could make an aspiration. You could use your own words or repeat a traditional aspiration, such as the *Four Limitless Ones* or the *Bodhisattva Vow*. (Refer to the "Daily Chants" section on p. 124.)

Sometimes you may feel that the formal practice of tonglen is too much for you. In that case, you could simply make the aspiration: "One day may I be able to open my heart a little more than I can today." With this approach, there is no blame or self-recrimination. There is just a sincere wish to grow.

EQUALITY PRACTICE

Equality practice is a way of connecting with others and realizing that you and they are in the same boat. It is a simple human truth that everyone, just like you, wants to be happy and to avoid suffering. Just like you, everyone else wants to have friends, to be accepted and loved, to be respected and valued for their unique qualities, to be healthy and to feel comfortable with themselves. Just like you, no one else wants to be friendless and alone, to be looked down upon by others, to be sick, to feel inadequate and depressed.

The equality practice is simply to remember this fact whenever you meet another person. You think, "Just like me, she wants to be happy; she doesn't want to suffer." You might choose to practice this for a whole day, or maybe for just an hour or fifteen minutes. I really appreciate this practice, because it lifts the barrier of indifference to other people's joy, to their private pain, and to their wonderful uniqueness.

In *The Way of the Bodhisattva*, the great Indian teacher and poet *Shantideva* stresses the importance of meditating on the equality of self and others in this way:

> Strive at first to meditate
> Upon the sameness of yourself and others.
> In joy and sorrow all are equal.
> Thus be guardian of all, as of yourself.

Jeffrey Hopkins, the Dalai Lama's translator for ten years, tells a story about travelling with him in the West. Wherever he went, His Holiness would repeat in English, "Everyone wants happiness, doesn't want suffering." He would go to an airport or a lecture hall or a news conference and say, "Everyone wants happiness, doesn't want suffering." At first Jeffrey thought, "Why does he keep saying this?" because it seemed so simplistic and ordinary. But after a while the message began to sink in, and he thought, "Yes, I need that!" It is simple, but it is also profoundly true, and it was exactly the kind of teaching he needed to hear.

At first, this practice might seem commonplace or shallow to you. But believe me, it's a real eye-opener. It humbles us, because it shines a spotlight on our habit of thinking that we are the center of the world. When we acknowledge our shared humanity with another person, we connect with them in a surprisingly intimate way. They become like family to us, and this helps dissolve our isolation and aloneness.

SHARING YOUR HEART

The practice of sharing your heart is twofold: sharing happiness and accepting pain. For the first, when anything is delightful in your life, you wish that other people could share it. For the second, when you feel any sense of suffering, you think that many other people are also suffering and you wish that they could be free from it. This is the very essence of the tonglen outlook: when things are pleasant, think of others; when things are painful, think of others. If this practice is the only thing you remember after reading this book, it will benefit you and everyone you come in contact with.

sharing happiness

When you experience any kind of pleasure or well-being in your life—appreciating a bright spring day, a good meal, a cute baby animal, or a nice hot shower—notice it and cherish it. Such simple pleasures can bring us a lot of joy, tenderness, and a sense of relief. We have many of these fleeting golden moments in our life, but we usually speed right past them. So the first part of the practice is just to stop, notice, and fully appreciate them. Next, you make the wish that other people could also enjoy them. As you do this practice more, you will probably find yourself noticing these moments of happiness and contentment more and more.

When you practice giving in this way, you don't bypass your own pleasure or enjoyment. Say you're eating a bowl of delicious strawberries. You don't think, "Oh, I shouldn't really be enjoying these so much. Think of all the other people who don't even have a piece of bread to eat." Instead, you should think, "Wow! This is a fantastic strawberry. I've never tasted anything so delicious." You can enjoy your strawberry thoroughly. But then you think, "I wish everyone could enjoy this, I hope that they will have a chance to enjoy this too."

You could also think of a personal possession that gives you a lot of pleasure, such as your favorite sweater or your favorite tie, then imagine giving it away to people you meet. This practice isn't about actually giving anything away, because you are working at the level of imagination. But it puts you in touch with your habit of grasping, shutting down, and not wanting to share things with others. In the process, you develop confidence in your own inherent richness, that fact that you always have a lot to give others.

Treya Wilbur described this kind of giving practice in the book *Grace and Grit*, which is about her battle with terminal cancer. She had already been doing tonglen for a long time. One day she lost a gold star necklace that her parents had given her, which was like a good-luck charm because she had worn it through all her most difficult times, chemotherapy and operations. When she couldn't find it anywhere, it seemed like a bad omen and she became depressed. But based on her experience of tonglen, she suddenly got the idea of visualizing millions of these stars and giving them away to benefit everyone she met. During the process of practicing in this way, she became acutely aware of her habitual patterns of desire, attachment, and clinging, and she began to give away anything for which she felt a momentary attachment. This didn't always help her to overcome her clinging, but through this work she developed compassion for everyone else like her who had good intentions but couldn't quite live up to them. Through this practice that she discovered through her own insight, she was able to get over losing the star and, most importantly, learned the joy of dropping attachment and giving to others.

accepting pain

The second part of the practice is somewhat more advanced. So don't try it unless you feel comfortable with the idea. First you notice when you experience something that is uncomfortable, painful, or unpleasant. Then you make the wish that other people could be completely free of it and imagine sending them whatever you think would bring relief.

For example, if you start to feel depressed, you say to yourself, "Since I'm feeling depressed anyway, may I accept it fully so that other people can be free of it." Or, "Since I have a toothache anyway, may I accept it completely so that other people may be free of it." Then send them a sense of relief. Just do it very simply, without worrying too much about the logic.

For many people, this kind of exchange will

seem like too much, too soon. But I present it
anyway, because I have personally found it very
empowering. It turns around the revulsion and
paranoia that we normally feel about anything unpleasant, the feeling that we are the target, and we
use it as fuel for awakening the heart.

"Traffic jam tonglen" is a specific instance of
this practice. It's about working with all the uncomfortable feelings that you experience when
you are stuck in a traffic jam, or perhaps in a very
long line at the market: anger, resentment, restless-
ness, uptightness, fear of missing an appointment.
First you look around and realize that all the other
people stuck in the jam are feeling the same way
you do. Then you breathe in fully whatever you are
feeling and send out a sense of relaxation and relief, both for yourself and all the other people in
the traffic jam. You realize that, as human beings,
you are all in the same boat. Everyone is putting
up barriers and using the discomfort of the traffic
jam to feel more and more isolated. So you turn
the situation around, and it becomes your link
with all the other people stuck in their cars. Suddenly, as you look out the window at them, they all
become human beings.

TONGLEN ON THE SPOT

This practice is really the essence of the tonglen approach. Because I have found it very helpful for myself, I like to recommend it to all my students. Even if you choose not to do the formal tonglen practice, you can always do this on-the-spot practice. Once you get used to it and practice it regularly, it will make formal tonglen practice more real and meaningful to you.

This is a practice that you can do for a real-life situation you meet in daily life. Whenever you meet a situation that awakens your compassion or that is painful and difficult for you, you can stop for a moment, breathe in any suffering that you see, and breathe out a sense of relief. It is a simple and direct process. Unlike the formal practice, it does not involve any visualizations or steps. It's a simple and natural exchange: you see suffering, you take it in with the inbreath, you send out relief with the outbreath.

For example, you might be in the supermarket and see a mother slapping her little girl. It is painful for you to see, but there is really nothing you can say or do at that moment. Your first reaction might be to turn away out of fear and try to forget it. But in this practice, instead of turning away, you could actually start to do tonglen for the little girl who is crying and also for the angry mother who has reached the end of her rope. You can send out a general sense of relaxation and openness or something specific, like a hug or a kind word, or whatever feels right to you at the moment. It's not all that conceptual; it's almost spontaneous. When you contact a painful situation in this way and stay with it, it can open up your heart and become the source of compassion.

You can do tonglen on the spot when strong emotions come up and you don't know what to do with them. For example, you might be having a painful argument with your spouse or your boss at work. They are yelling at you and you don't know how to react. So you can start to breathe in the painful feelings and send out a sense of spaciousness and relaxation with the outbreath—for yourself, for the person who is yelling at you, and for all the other people who are dealing with a similar difficult situation. Of course, at some point you have to react to the person who is yelling at you but, by introducing some space and warmth into the situation, you will probably deal with it more skillfully.

You can also do this practice when you feel some blockage to opening and developing compassion. For example, you see a homeless person on the street who is asking you for money and seems to be an alcoholic. In spite of your desire to be compassionate, you can't help but turn away and feel disgust or resentment. At that point, you can start doing tonglen for yourself and all the other people who want to be open but are basically shut down. You breathe in the feeling of shut-downness, your own and everybody else's. Then you send out a sense of space or relaxation or letting go. When you feel blocked, that's not an obstacle to tonglen; it's part of the practice. You work with what feels like blockage as the seed of awakening your heart and as connection with other people.

TONGLEN ON THE STREET

This practice is to walk down the street, perhaps for just one or two blocks, with the intention of staying as open as possible to whoever you meet. It is a training in being more emotionally honest with yourself and being more emotionally available to others. As you are walking, you could relax your posture and have the feeling that the area of your heart and chest is open. As you pass people, you might even feel a subtle connection between their heart and yours, as if the two of you were linked by an invisible cord. You could think to yourself, "May you be happy," as you pass them. The main point is to feel a sense of interconnectedness with all the people you meet.

If you are feeling somewhat exposed and embarrassed by doing the practice, just acknowledge it and realize that other people are probably feeling the same way. You may notice how people glance briefly at you as they approach — usually at a safe distance, so it isn't obvious — in an automatic gesture of reaching out. Perhaps they are looking for someone who would be friendly to them and say hello, someone they could genuinely connect with. Sound familiar?

As you encounter each person, acknowledge your thoughts and emotional reactions toward them. Notice if you feel a sense of attachment, aversion, or indifference toward the people you pass. But don't add any self-judgement on top of it. You might see someone smiling, which could cheer you up on the spot and make you open further. Or you might see someone looking depressed, which could spark feelings of tenderness and compassion.

Notice when you begin to shut down or open up. But if you do find yourself shutting down, you don't blame yourself. You can simply empathize with all the people who are shutting down in the same way and aspire to be more and more open. Also, if you feel a sense of delight or pleasure on your walk, you could wish to share it with the people you meet.

STEPPING INTO OTHERS' SHOES

This practice of exchanging yourself with others is presented in Shantideva's *The Way of the Bodhisattva*. It is more of a contemplation and, unlike tonglen, it isn't synchronized with the in- and outbreath. It can help you open up to, and empathize with, the so-called neutral or indifferent people in your life, as well as those you find really difficult.

First imagine the person you are working with as vividly as possible. Be very inquisitive and spend some time really trying to stand in their shoes and see the world as they do. What do they feel? What do they want? What do they fear? Just taking this much interest in a person can go a long way in developing appreciation and concern for them.

To take it a step further, think that you are them and they are you. You are standing in their shoes and you are now looking at yourself as the other person sees you. How do they see you? As just a neutral person, as a potential friend, as an enemy, as an arrogant person, as a warm person? What would they like for you to give them: a hug, an encouraging word, an open and attentive ear, appreciation for their intelligence and their talents, an apology, forgiveness?

By trading places, you discover that what the other person wants is pretty much the same as what you want. In that way, you are equals. Perhaps you also discover that you have never really seen them or heard them before, that you haven't appreciated them or treated them fairly. Based on this new understanding, you may open to them more the next time you see them.

tonglen on the cushion

In cultivating bodhichitta, sitting meditation and tonglen always go hand in hand. Although sitting and tonglen are intimately connected, they are different in their approach. Sitting is basically nonconceptual; it notices thoughts and emotions and then lets go of them. Tonglen actually uses concepts, images, memories, and emotions to develop compassion.

In sitting meditation, you train in seeing the dreamlike and nonsubstantial nature of whatever arises in your mind—your personal dramas, hopes and fears, plans and fantasies, and mental strategies for gaining comfort and security—and letting go of words and concepts. You are looking at thoughts and emotions more from the perspective of absolute bodhichitta and *shunyata*. Sitting meditation is a very profound method, but it has a potential drawback. In a subtle and unconscious way, you could use the practice to avoid looking deeply at unwanted thoughts and emotions or to suppress them, in order to achieve a feeling of peace and tranquillity.

Tonglen is more conceptual than sitting meditation. It is more like a contemplative practice. You could say that it is more proactive, because you use thoughts and images to kindle the practice. You actually invite or provoke unwanted feelings in order to work with them. First you use words and images to get in touch with strong emotions and memories. Then you drop the words and use emotions and memory as a method for awakening compassion. Unlike sitting meditation, you are not trying to look at thoughts and emotions from an absolute point of view and seeing them all as ungraspable and nonsubstantial. Instead, you're grappling with real-life issues, working with all the ways you ordinarily get stuck.

Of course, sitting and tonglen are similar in many ways. For both, you are sitting on a meditation cushion, either in your own room or in a meditation hall with other people. The environment is relatively quiet and safe, so that you can afford to relax and work with your mind and heart. Good posture is important for both. In tonglen, you follow the same *six points of good posture* as for sitting meditation, but for tonglen your eyes can be opened or closed.

In general, you should be very familiar with sitting meditation before you begin to do tonglen on the cushion. (Tonglen on the spot is another matter, however. You can do it any time in your daily life when it feels right.) Sitting is an essential foundation for tonglen, because it develops stability of mind, the ability to stay in the present moment with whatever arises. So it is highly recommended to sit just before and after doing a session of tonglen. For example, you could sit for twenty minutes, do tonglen for ten to fifteen minutes, and end with another twenty minutes of sitting.

When Trungpa Rinpoche first introduced the practice, his students used to do tonglen for half an hour at a time, but I have discovered that this is very demanding for most people. Currently I suggest that people do it for about ten to fifteen minutes at a stretch, but this is not a strict rule. If you

feel comfortable with the practice and are inspired
to do it longer, that's fine. Group tonglen practice is
usually scheduled for no more than fifteen minutes.

MAKING A LIST

No matter how much spontaneous compassion
they may feel in their daily life, some people "dry
up" when they begin tonglen. As soon as the bell
rings, their minds go blank and they can't think of
any subject for their practice. For this reason, I
suggest that you keep a running list of people, animals, or situations that you would like to include
in your practice. By recalling names on the list,
you can tap into the feelings of loving-kindness
and compassion that you already have, right now,
as a basis for further extending bodhichitta.

You could make two lists. One could be labeled
"love and gratitude"; the other, "compassion." For
the first list, think about people that you naturally
feel love or gratitude toward, people you cherish.
Whenever you think about them, you naturally
tap into a free-flowing feeling of love, gratitude,
and tenderness. The name on the list doesn't have
to be a person; it could be an animal. It could also

be someone close to you who has died. It might be someone you met only once but you will never forget because of the great kindness they showed you when you really needed it. It could even be someone you have never met but has been such a tremendous inspiration to your life that you feel you know them intimately. Don't be discouraged if you can't come up with anybody at first. Just keep your mind open. Even one name on the list is good enough.

On the second list are people or animals toward whom you naturally feel compassion whenever you think of them. Compassion is a spontaneous and heartfelt wish to alleviate their pain and suffering, whether physical or mental. You can list individuals or a general category, such as abused children, animals used for laboratory experiments, or people dying of AIDS or cancer.

As a young boy in Tibet, Trungpa Rinpoche once looked down from the top of his monastery and saw a group of people stoning a puppy and jeering. After that, he only had to think of that puppy in order to activate his compassion during tonglen. The main point is to touch into anything that genuinely brings out the compassion you already have.

THE FOUR STAGES

When you do tonglen as a formal meditation practice, it has four stages:

1   Flashing a sense of openness
2   Working with the textures of claustrophobia and freshness
3   Working with specific people or situations in your life
4   Expanding the practice out to others

To begin a session, check that you have good posture. You can take a moment to review the six points of posture. Feel that your body is firmly planted on the earth and that your head is connected with the sky above. A broad and open chest will help you contact the tender-hearted qualities of love and compassion.

stage one

The first stage is flashing a sense of openness—open heart and open mind. This lasts for just a few seconds. Traditionally it is called "flashing absolute bodhichitta." One of the lojong slogans, "Rest in the nature of alaya, the essence," is connected with this stage, where alaya refers to the ultimate open and spacious nature of mind.

The intention of flashing openness is to recognize that a lot of space is always available to us, at any moment of time. Even in the middle of warfare, in the middle of domestic violence, in the middle of famine, there is always space if we can just acknowledge it. One image for this openness is the vast blue sky. Even when it is hidden by thick, dark clouds, the blue sky is always there. So the purpose of this stage is to connect us with that large view of things, like an astronaut's view of the earth from outer space.

To contact the feeling of openness, some people like to use an image, such as looking into the clear blue sky or standing on the shore of a vast ocean. Some people recall being high in the mountains and looking out over miles and miles of uninterrupted landscape. Others like to think of being in an airplane and looking out the window at the vast world of clouds and sky. You can use any image that evokes a sense of spaciousness and of not being caught up in your narrow world.

One woman I know used an especially humorous image. First she imagined that everyone in the meditation hall had a speech balloon, like the ones you see in cartoons, which was filled with all their thoughts. Then she imagined that, at exactly the same time, everyone labeled their thoughts as thinking and the balloons dissolved spontaneously. This left a very profound sense of stillness: a quiet room made even more quiet by the disappearance of all thinking.

When you are practicing with a group, you can flash openness and rest your mind when you hear the sound of the bell. The time it takes for the sound of the bell to die down is about the right length of time for flashing openness.

The step of flashing openness, or absolute bodhichitta, is quite brief. But in some sense it is the very aim and essence of the practice. Our aspiration is to be open and not to close down in all the situations of our life, no matter how difficult. So it is necessary to connect with the possibility of this openness from the very beginning. Then, when we start to work with painful situations in the practice, they are less likely to overwhelm us because we know—intellectually, at least—that they all take place within a more vast space. If we get bogged down in the practice, we could flash back to the first stage for an instant. In fact, it would be good if we could take the initial moment of openness and stretch out that feeling, so to speak, through all the other stages.

stage two

In the second stage, we synchronize the in-breath with the qualities of claustrophobia and stuckness and the outbreath with the qualities of freshness and spaciousness. The eyes can be either opened or closed. When we breathe in, we feel the textures of hot, dark, heavy, thick, and cramped; when we breathe out, we feel the textures of light, cool, peaceful, and refreshing. This process has to do with textures, feelings, and moods; it is not at all conceptual. Working with textures helps us to get in touch with the felt qualities of claustrophobia and spaciousness. Once we contact the feelings, we can let go of the words and concepts— "dark" and "light," "hot" and "cool."

At this point, you could manipulate your breathing a little, if you find that it helps. You can breathe in and out deeply. This is different than the instructions for shamatha-vipashyana, where we simply observe our ordinary breath, whether it is fast or slow, deep or shallow, and do not try to control it in any way. But for tonglen, it is fine to

regulate the breath a little. The main point is to
breathe in the quality of claustrophobia completely and fully, and to send out the quality of refreshing spaciousness completely and fully.

In tonglen, the inbreath and outbreath are mu-
tually interdependent. The more you can breathe
in and open the heart when you ordinarily would
close it, the more there will be to send out to
others. And the more you can connect with the
feelings of spaciousness, kindness, love, and cheerfulness, the more strength you will have to take in
what is unpleasant.

Try to spend an equal amount of time on the
inbreath and the outbreath. People usually tend to
emphasize one or the other. On the one hand—
strangely enough—you might feel quite comfortable with the claustrophobia, heaviness, and unpleasant feelings, and so breathe them in very
deeply. But you might feel very poverty-stricken,
thinking that you don't have anything to send out,
and so let out a teeny-weeny outbreath. On the
other hand, you might feel afraid to take in too
much pain or pollution, and so breathe in very
quickly—whhht!—and let out a very long, refreshing, and delightful outbreath.

The traditional instruction is to breathe the textures in and out of all the pores of your body, 360 degrees in all directions, as well as above and below. This method emphasizes a sense of breathing environmentally. It helps to overcome the feeling that you are concentrating all the "bad stuff" into one small area of your body. As you breathe in, you might feel afraid that you are taking in something painful or harmful to your system. This can result in a feeling of tightness and heaviness in the area of the heart. Having an infinite number of breathing holes helps you to feel that there is no single place for the "bad stuff" to get stuck. Then, on the outbreath, this method gives the feeling that you are sending out all the "good stuff" very spaciously and generously in all directions.

One method of working with the feeling of being overwhelmed is to expand the heart as wide as it needs to be in order to accommodate whatever is coming in. Another method is to think of your body as hollow and spacious, like a balloon, rather than being made out of solid flesh and bones. Or you could think of your body as a hologram, completely transparent and made of light. The most important point is to use an image—whether an infinitely expanding heart, a hollow body, or a hologram — that gives you confidence that there is no place for anything to get stuck.

You continue the second stage until you feel that your breathing and the visualization of textures are comfortably synchronized. But don't dwell on it too long. Stage three is really the main part of the practice. Generally speaking, you wouldn't spend more than a third of the session — if even that much — on stage two.

If you get bogged down during stage three, you could return to stage two and work with textures for a minute, if that helps.

Some people find it difficult to connect with stage two, because it seems too abstract. If this is true for you, after you have become very familiar with the practice, you could choose to shorten the amount of time you spend on it.

stage three

The third stage involves working with a particular situation, one that is very personal and real to you, and using it to develop further compassion. By tapping into the memory of a situation where you already feel compassion, you learn to open your heart further. You could think of a person, animal, or group that is on your list, or it could be someone who comes immediately to mind. If it helps, you could visualize their face clearly in front of you, or just think that they are really present. In your imagination, you could even address them by name and say something to express your caring for them, such as "May you be happy" or "I love you."

Once you have begun, you might find that you start thinking of many other people, one after the other. That's no problem. You can do the exchange for each of them as they arise.

As you breathe in, you take in whatever suffering they might be experiencing. As you breathe out, you send out whatever you feel might heal them. If it helps, you could imagine a smile or some other sign of relief on the person's face as you breathe in their suffering and breathe out relief.

Just as for the second stage, if you like, you can manipulate your breath somewhat, breathing in and out slowly and deeply. Again, it is important to spend an equal amount of time on the inbreath and outbreath. Some people find it difficult to visualize the exchange of taking and sending on a single breath. Doing a lot of tonglen on the spot will probably solve this problem. But if necessary,

you could spend a few breaths to take in the sense
of suffering and a few breaths to send out relief
and happiness.

You can send out something very general, such
as a sense of opening and spaciousness, or something a little more specific, such as love, forgiveness, a sense of humor, or joy. You can send something very concrete, such as a delicious meal, a
soothing bath, a beautiful sunset, a good cup of
coffee, or a warm hug—whatever you think would
make the other person happy. But try not to be
too analytical. If you try to figure out precisely
what would relieve the other person's suffering
and make them happy at this very moment, the
practice may become just a conceptual exercise. In
this case, your first thought is probably the best
thought.

If you are doing tonglen for someone who is
seriously ill, such as a person with cancer or AIDS,
it is important to understand that you are not doing the practice to physically remove their disease.
You are doing it with the wish to relieve them of
the emotional suffering that surrounds their disease: their fear, their anger, their resentment, their
shame, their despair. Fundamentally, you are wishing to offer them space enough to relax and con-

nect with their own heart—their wisdom, their strength, their sense of humor and delight—so that, by a sudden shift in attitude, they can drop their sense of burden.

You don't have to start the exchange by thinking of another person. You can start with what you are feeling right in the present moment. This was actually Trungpa Rinpoche's instruction when he first presented the practice to his students. He said to use anything difficult that is coming up right now in your life as an object for tonglen. It doesn't have to be a major trauma; it could just be a minor irritation. In fact, it is helpful to start with smaller things, because they aren't overwhelming, and then your capacity to work with more difficult things will grow naturally.

Trungpa Rinpoche said that you use whatever you are feeling in this moment as a steppingstone for understanding that other people are in the same boat. When you breathe in and fully acknowledge and accept what you're feeling, your particular feeling of discomfort no longer causes you to become more isolated, more self-involved, and more needing to protect yourself. Instead, your discomfort becomes your link to all the other people who are feeling uncomfortable.

For example, if you are feeling resentment, you could call up the image of the person or the memory of a situation that vividly connects you with the resentment. You breathe in and connect fully with the resentment, then you send out a feeling of relief and expansiveness with the outbreath—both to yourself and to everyone else who is feeling resentment.

When you start by working with a personal issue, it is very important to remember that you are not practicing for yourself alone. In effect, you are using what you are feeling in the present moment as a steppingstone to understand, empathize with, and develop genuine compassion for others. So in a sense, you are breathing in and out for yourself and for others at the same time.

With this kind of understanding, you "don't wallow in self-pity," as one lojong slogan says. In other words, you don't dwell excessively on your own feelings. You fully acknowledge them as your own, but at the same time you recognize that you share them with your brothers and sisters on the planet. This recognition alone is quite liberating; it can bring you real personal relief. At the same time, you completely know what other people are up against, and then your heart opens up to them.

In this way, you can fully own the feelings as your experience without denying or repressing them. But at the same time, in some sense you are disowning them as your unique personal possession.

Over the years, the way I have taught stage three has evolved. At first, I used to tell people to do tonglen with themselves as the reference point. Students would often tell me how healing the practice was for themselves. But when I asked, "How about other people?" they would answer, "Oh! I forgot the part about other people." So then I started to teach the practice in the more traditional way, which is just doing it for other people. Then students told me that they felt they had entered dangerous waters, because it would bring up a lot of fear and resistance for them. When I asked if they did tonglen for themselves and others in the same boat, they were shocked and said, "Oh! I didn't know that I could do it for myself." Those seem to be the two principal extremes: doing the practice only for yourself or doing it for others but reaching a point where you can't do it at all.

As a middle way, I currently teach students to start doing tonglen for others, such as someone on their list. If they have a natural feeling of compassion for the other person and can do tonglen for them wholeheartedly, that is all they need to do during most of the session. But this is a key point that I now emphasize: When you start to have difficulty in doing the practice, you can always shift your focus and begin doing tonglen for the obstacle you are feeling, with the simultaneous recognition that other people are experiencing the same sort of obstacle.

For example, you may start to do tonglen for a particular person with a wholehearted intention to help them, but suddenly it becomes complicated. There are many possible scenarios. Perhaps you become afraid of taking in more pain than you can handle. Perhaps you are overwhelmed with sadness or grief. Perhaps you have an emotionally ambiguous relationship with the other person, such as a parent or spouse: you are actually very resentful toward the very person you wanted to help. Or perhaps you feel like a failure; you feel completely poverty-stricken that you have nothing to offer others. In any case, you feel that you can't continue the practice because it evokes emotions that seem negative, inappropriate, or overpowering.

At that point, you should not think that your tonglen is a failure. On the contrary, you have successfully contacted a tender and alive issue that you can work with. At this point, you just shift the object of your attention. Breathe in and completely acknowledge whatever seems to be an obstacle—your fear, your sadness, your irritation, or your sense of failure. You feel its heaviness and your tendency to shut down around it, then you open your heart to your own shut-down feelings.

When you breathe in, you let go of the words and the story line. At the beginning, the story line puts you in touch with the naked energy of the emotions. This energy is a palpable quality in the body and has nothing to do with words. So you drop the story line and go directly into the energy through working with the in- and outbreath.

In brief, when your heart starts to shut down, you completely acknowledge what you're feeling as the basis of nurturing compassion. Next, you recognize that many other people in the world are feeling exactly what you are feeling, so you can feel genuine empathy for them. Finally, you send out to yourself and all others whatever you think will help.

stage four

In stage four, you universalize the practice. You start out with a feeling of compassion that is not theoretical; it is completely real, specific, immediate, and heartfelt to you. Then you expand it out to others as far as you can. In stage three, you begin by doing tonglen for the pain of someone you know or for your own personal distress. In stage four, you recognize and appreciate that this pain is an experience shared by many, if not all, human beings on this planet. In this way, what starts out as very relative and personal and immediate to you becomes your connection with all beings.

For example, you might be doing stage three for a little child who breaks your heart and whose suffering you would like to alleviate. You could expand that sense of heartbreak and compassion to all the other children who are in a similar situation. Then you could expand it to all children who are suffering. If it feels real to you, you could expand it even further to the suffering of all beings.

The fourth stage could be almost simultaneous with stage three. As you breathe in with the wish to help a particular person, at the same time you could think that you are breathing in for all the other people in the same situation. Then you send out a sense of relief to the particular person and to all the others.

RETURNING TO SITTING PRACTICE

For group practice, when the bell rings to end tonglen, you return to sitting meditation. If you like, as the sound of the bell dies out, you could think of radiating out white light—cool, peaceful, and refreshing—to all sentient beings without exception. You could also make the aspiration: "May all sentient beings enjoy happiness and root of happiness. May they be free from suffering and the root of suffering."

Finally, when the bell has completely rung out, you deliberately let all thoughts and images drop away. You could readjust your posture and begin applying the technique of sitting meditation. Usually you would sit for at least fifteen minutes after finishing tonglen.

There are many approaches to practicing tonglen. After thoroughly becoming familiar with the basic technique in four stages, you should feel free to make the practice your own. In order to be real and touch your heart, it needs to become completely personal. This chapter presents a number of variations on the technique that you could experiment with. Use only the ones that really work for you. In other words, choose the best and leave the rest.

VARIOUS TOPICS

The following is a list of possible topics for stage three of tonglen that will give you an idea of the tremendous variety possible. As always, no matter what subject you begin with, you would universalize the exchange during stage four.

Your own pain at this moment, either physical or psychological

A personal craving or addiction

A habitual pattern that is very strong

A difficult situation that you are presently facing in your life

A painful memory, either recent or ancient

Yourself as a child

Your own feeling of blockage with the practice

A member of your family

Your spouse or partner

Someone you naturally hold dear, such as your own child

Someone you feel very grateful toward, such as a teacher or mentor

Someone you naturally have compassion for, such as an injured child or animal

A friend or neighbor

Someone that you know is having a hard time
   right now in their life

A class of people or animals that are suffering,
   such as laboratory animals, people with cancer
   or AIDS, famine victims, abused children,
   people suffering in war-torn countries

Someone close to you who has died

Someone close to you who is seriously ill

Someone whom you feel neutral toward; that is,
   you barely know them and usually would not
   even think of them

Someone whose suffering you have read about in
   the newspapers or seen on television.

Someone whose suffering you have read in a book
   or seen in a film, for example, the persecution
   of Jews in *Schindler's List*.

Someone who is suffering but for whom you have
   a hard time feeling compassion, for example,
   an abusive alcoholic

Someone who has hurt you, physically or
   emotionally

A difficult person in your life, like your boss or
   someone else at work

A difficult relationship between yourself and
   another person; this is not specifically for

yourself or for the other person, but for the relationship as a whole

EXPANDING THE HEART

This is a method that may alleviate the feeling that you are taking in too much and are overwhelmed. As you breathe in for stages two and three, you can imagine that your heart opens as wide as necessary to accommodate what you find unpleasant or poisonous, and you let it in completely. As you breathe out, either from all the pores of your body or from your heart, you send out refreshing openness. You breathe in as fearlessly as you can, then send out as much generosity and expansiveness as you can. This method deliberately opens up the heart area, like opening and relaxing a tight muscle.

DISSOLVING THE BARRIERS

This is an alternative visualization for stage two of the practice that is found in Sogyal Rinpoche's book, *The Tibetan Book of Living and Dying*. When you breathe in, you imagine that the suffering of others enters your heart as black smoke and dissolves the hard armor surrounding it. The armor is a good image for the barriers of ego-clinging. When the armor is penetrated and dissolved by the blackness, the cool white light of compassion automatically streams from the heart. This is a powerful way to do the practice, because the image gets to the root of how tonglen works: by dissolving ego's barriers, compassion naturally arises.

STARTING THE FLOW

Although it is not usually a part of tonglen instruction, some people find that it helps to get the feeling of compassion flowing from the very beginning of the session—priming the pump of compassion, as it were. It makes the whole practice seem much more real for them. As soon as the bell rings to begin tonglen, you could start by reflecting on something that breaks your heart, like an animal in the zoo, a child that has been mistreated, or a friend with cancer. This may help you to get in touch with your emotions and establish your motivation before starting.

SPONTANEOUS TONGLEN

You can do tonglen without choosing a particular subject at the beginning of the session. Instead, you can work with whatever comes up naturally. When it comes time to do tonglen, Trungpa Rinpoche said that you could continue sitting without searching for a topic. Then, as thoughts and emotions arise spontaneously, you work with whatever material presents itself. This method guarantees that you are working with something real and personal, rather than rehearsed and abstract.

If you would like to try this approach, you could begin your tonglen session with stages one and two, then just sit and wait for a subject to present itself. Of course, the problem with this method is that your mind may freeze and nothing will come up. If that happens, you can always fall back on your list of names.

WIDENING THE CIRCLE OF COMPASSION

This approach is similar to the maitri and compassion practices that are described later (see p. 119). First you begin by doing tonglen for yourself,

for a specific painful feeling or issue in your life.
Then you extend the practice step by step to others: someone for whom you already feel friendliness and compassion, someone you feel neutral or
indifferent toward, someone that you find difficult
to relate to, and finally all sentient beings.

When you begin to do the exchange for other
people, you could work with the same issue you
were using for yourself. For example, if you are
feeling very discouraged, you could take in the dis-
couragement of a close friend and send them out
confidence and a feeling of cheerfulness. Then you
could do exactly the same for a neutral person, a
difficult person, and for all people who are feeling
discouraged with their lives.

FACING YOURSELF

If you are doing tonglen for yourself, you could actually imagine yourself standing in front of yourself. Think of yourself in your own place and also
in front of you. Then do tonglen for yourself in
front, finally expanding it to others.

One variation of this is working with the issue

of shame and regret. It is adapted from instructions in *The Tibetan Book of Living and Dying.* Here we do tonglen for things we have done that we are ashamed of, which Sogyal Rinpoche describes as taking full responsibility for your own actions. When you come to the third stage, you think of something you have done that makes you wince. You breathe in and completely acknowledge your feelings about it: shame, embarrassment, denial, despair, or compulsively blaming yourself. Then you send out forgiveness and healing to yourself.

You can use the imagery of opening your heart wide enough to allow in all the unwanted feelings. If it helps, you can visualize yourself in front of yourself as you do the exchange.

Finally, you extend this exchange to others, which helps not to feel overwhelmed by the inbreath. Simultaneously with the third step, or as a separate fourth step, breathe in for both yourself and all other people who are feeling shame or embarrassment. Then send out forgiveness to yourself and others.

RADIATING COMPASSION

This practice is like dropping a pebble of compassion in a pool of water and watching the circle of waves radiate outward. Begin by doing tonglen for yourself. You can work with a specific personal issue or you can just think, "May I be happy, may I be free of suffering." Then begin to expand the practice outward from yourself: first to everyone in the same room, then to everyone in the same building, everyone in the neighborhood, everyone in your town, and finally to the nation and the whole world.

MAITRI BHAVANA

In the Buddhist tradition, many practices have a tonglen component. Two specific practices that use tonglen as their basis are the *Maitri Bhavana* and the *Sukhavati Ceremony*. Maitri Bhavana, which means "meditation on loving-kindness," is a practice for the seriously ill. It is usually done as a group, but you could do it individually for a relative or friend if you like. It is important to remember that, when we practice for the sick, we're not breathing in their actual disease, such as cancer or AIDS. Rather, we're breathing in their tendency to shut down and become paralyzed by pain—their despair, anger, resentment, denial, and feelings of isolation. Then we breathe out a sense of spaciousness and relaxation with the aspiration that their illness will become a genuine path of awakening for them, whether they recover or not. (For complete instructions on the Maitri Bhavana, see p. 130.)

SUKHAVATI

The Sukhavati Ceremony is a funeral ceremony that includes practicing tonglen for the person who has died. Through the practice, we allow the person the freedom to let go completely of their life. We breathe in their fear, confusion, regret, and attachment to their body and to habitual mental patterns. On the outbreath, we send out basic sanity, fearlessness, cheerfulness, and openness.

We shouldn't try to kid ourselves. Tonglen is a challenging practice, even for those who have done it for a long time. So don't become discouraged when you experience problems doing it. This is a practice for a lifetime, not just for a weekend or a week or a year. If you take the long-term perspective, you can afford to relax. There will be plenty of time to get the hang of it.

Bodhichitta is sometimes compared to the sun; our patterns of putting up barriers are like clouds that cover it. Like the sun, bodhichitta is always shining, so as the clouds begin to dissolve, our true nature shines through. I find this image very inspiring whenever I'm feeling that I'll never get unstuck. It's a reminder that openness of heart and mind is always available to us — right here, right now — even when we feel hopelessly shut-down. To uncover it, all we need is gentleness, kindness — and patience.

If the formal practice of tonglen seems too overwhelming, just trust your own instincts and don't push yourself. You could give up doing tonglen for the time being and do something different. You could just do sitting meditation as your formal practice, but also experiment with doing tonglen on the spot in your daily life. You could also try doing the practices of maitri and compassion (see p. 119) which people usually find easier than tonglen.

If you feel that tonglen is too much for you, I think that making aspirations is very helpful. It is a gentle approach and sows seeds for being able to do it in the future. You can just think, "One day may I be able to open my heart and mind a little more than I can today. One day may I be able to give to others more than I can today." Later on, you might find that the formal tonglen practice feels

right and is easier for you. It might seem very
natural and appropriate to do, for example, when
you're sitting with a friend who is very ill.

By all means, please don't do tonglen as a
"should" or an obligation, and don't feel like a failure if you can't do it right now. The practice is all
about developing unconditional friendliness and
compassion for yourself and others. So it makes
no sense to use it in order to give yourself a hard
time.

Whenever you get bogged down during a practice session, it is always fine to make a fresh start.
You could take a break and drop the technique altogether for a minute. Or you could clear the air
by flashing absolute bodhichitta and reconnecting
with a sense of openness and freshness. Then you
could return to stage two or go directly to stage
three, perhaps with a subject that is easier.

RECONNECTING WITH MOTIVATION

When you get stuck or lose inspiration, it is helpful to stop for a minute and think carefully about
your original motivation for doing the practice. In
fact, it would probably be a good idea to do this at

the beginning of every practice session. One way to reconnect with your motivation is by saying the Four Limitless Ones or the Bodhisattva Vow to yourself. Or you could recall the reason why you practice in your own words, such as:

> Our hearts are naturally open and compassionate,
> But because we fear painful emotions and situations,
> We create barriers to protect ourselves.
> In order to dissolve the barriers and open our hearts,
> We are willing to acknowledge and own the pain we feel
> And to ventilate it with loving-kindness and compassion.
> By relating to our own pain in an honest and compassionate way,
> We can open our hearts fully to others.

If you become bogged down in the details of the practice, you could briefly review the instructions in your own words, such as:

> When you notice that you're shutting down,
> Breathe in your pain and fully accept it.

Then relax, open, and soften.
Breathe out relief to yourself and all others
    who are feeling the same thing.

THE FOUR REMINDERS

Another way to reconnect with your motivation is
to contemplate the four reminders, sometimes
also called the "four ways of reversing our intention." They sum up our human condition and
point to the great importance of practicing
bodhichitta:

1   *The preciousness of being born as a human be-
    ing.* Bodhichitta is our birthright as human be-
    ings. We have healthy faculties, a tender heart,
    and good intelligence. On top of that, we have
    been very fortunate to connect with teachings
    about bodhichitta, which explain how to over-
    come the barriers to being fully alive and open.

2   *The shortness of life.* We all know that we will
    die sooner or later, but we have no idea when it
    will be. Usually we kid ourselves by thinking
    that we will have enough time to accomplish
    everything we want to accomplish, and so we

procrastinate. But we could die tomorrow. Before we die, nothing is more meaningful than overcoming fear, opening our hearts, and experiencing the joy of a shared humanity. So we should start today.

3 *We reap what we sow through our actions.* Everything that happens in our lives today is the result of our previous thoughts, words, and deeds. And whatever we do today will have a positive or negative effect in the future. If we practice bodhichitta, we are sowing seeds for awakening love and compassion—both for ourselves and the world. If we don't, we will continue to strengthen our emotional barriers and consequently experience tremendous struggle and frustration in our lives.

4 *Suffering is inherent in just being alive.* As soon as we're born, pain is inevitable. We will grow old, get sick, and die. But pain itself is not the real problem. Needless suffering comes from shutting down to pain, shutting down our own feelings, shutting off from others. By practicing bodhichitta, we can actually do something to heal this kind of suffering.

USING OBSTACLES AS THE PATH

As I have said before—and this really can't be said enough—if you are having any problem doing the practice, you can always begin doing tonglen for the obstacle you are feeling. At that point, don't think that your tonglen has failed. You just shift the object of your attention. No matter what the obstacle is, you breathe it in and accept it as your own. You also recognize that a lot of other people in the world are feeling exactly what you are feeling. Then you send out to yourself and others whatever you think will help. You can use this approach as a universal antidote for any kind of obstacle that you are experiencing.

This approach is similar to the lojong slogan, "Correct all wrongs with one intention." In general, the slogan means to meet every situation, no matter how difficult, with the intention to decrease self-centeredness and to increase bodhichitta. Here, in particular, it means to acknowledge whatever you experience as an obstacle for your tonglen practice, to embrace it fully, and to use it as a stepping stone for connecting with others.

FIVE COMMON OBSTACLES

There are several obstacles that almost always come up for people when they are practicing tonglen:

Becoming totally distracted by thoughts
Feeling overwhelmed by strong emotions
Feeling emotionally numb
Fear of being polluted
Not knowing what to send out

becoming totally distracted by thoughts

Sometimes people become so distracted by thoughts and emotions that they can't remember where they are or what they're doing on the cushion. This is not surprising. In tonglen we actually provoke thoughts, memories, and emotions as a basis for experiencing genuine feelings of compassion. But sometimes the storylines take on a life of their own and we seem powerless to stop them.

According to Trungpa Rinpoche, whenever you become distracted during a session, the antidote is the same as for sitting meditation: you can just stop and then start fresh. It would also be good to check your posture and correct it if necessary, since body and mind are intimately connected.

If you are frequently distracted, it would be good to do more sitting meditation before tonglen. Sitting helps to stabilize the mind so that you can stay more in the present moment. Relaxing your body can also be helpful, since wild thoughts tend to go along with physical uptightness. Breathing more deeply and regularly is a natural way to relax.

feeling overwhelmed by strong emotions

People who do tonglen tend to fall into two categories. Some people become overwhelmed by the powerful raw emotions that come up, either their own pain or others' suffering, and break down crying or have to stop practicing. Others become numb and can't feel anything.

We had a running joke at one of our lojong retreats at Gampo Abbey. When the bell rang to begin tonglen, certain people would start crying, just like clockwork. After a while, we started passing around boxes of Kleenex as soon as the bell rang. We always had about a dozen boxes in the meditation hall just in case. Later, when I interviewed the participants, one group felt very embarrassed about how emotional they were and wished they could be more disciplined. The other group felt very bad because they felt no emotions whatsoever; they would have paid anything to burst into tears during a session. So each group was being hard on itself and wanted to switch places with the other.

When you are feeling overwhelmed, you have to judge for yourself when to pull back and go more slowly. This guideline goes along with the slogan, "Of the two witnesses, hold the principal one." In other words, you yourself are the principal witness, and you need to trust your own instincts: you need to go at your own speed and to practice kindness and gentleness. If you try to be macho, the practice will backfire on you: you will shut down and give it up altogether. A gentle approach is absolutely essential but, at the same time, you aspire to be able to step more and more into tender areas and into groundlessness.

Tonglen is a practice of opening the heart and mind by relating with pain in a new way, using it as a seed of maitri for yourself and of compassion for others. But if you don't know how to swim, you don't have to dive into the deep end of the swimming pool. You can choose subjects that are easier and more workable for you, subjects that are heartfelt but not overwhelming, such as daily minor irritations or the misfortune of someone you just met.

For example, a woman wrote to me about trying to do the practice for her son, who was a heroin addict. When she did it for her son, she found it overwhelming; she also found it overwhelming to do it for other families in her situation. But she really wanted to get into the practice. Then he saw a story on television about the local football team that had lost a game. So she decided to do tonglen for the losing team. To her surprise, she discovered that she could actually handle it. After that experience, her confidence began to grow so that she could do the practice for anything.

Once your heart starts to open, it naturally opens to more and more difficult situations. That's why I sometimes say that the practice works through magic or grace. Of course, it does take some effort at the beginning to connect with your heart. But at some point the heart takes over and starts to evolve by itself.

Although gentleness and going at your own pace is essential, it's important to remember that tonglen isn't about avoiding pain. One time a student asked Trungpa Rinpoche, "How do you give your best when you feel your worst?" Rinpoche's answer was that you go deeper and deeper into the feeling of "worst." That sounds like a pretty tough order, but that's what tonglen is really about— being willing to move closer to our pain. It means developing the confidence and bravery to sit for maybe just one more second with something you previously thought was impossible to stay with.

When you connect with the vividness of pain, it is important to have a sense of "no big deal." Pain is just ordinary pain. Of course, you don't try to deny or repress the realness of pain. But you realize that it's not all that dramatic or monolithic, and it contains a lot of space and openness. This is using the view of absolute bodhichitta—which could also be called "absolute no-big-dealness"— as a remedy.

When you feel overwhelmed, the attention often shifts from thinking about another person's pain to your own fear of pain like theirs. So one instruction is to keep returning gently to an awareness of the other person's suffering, connecting with it as fully as possible, instead of becoming lost in self-involved fear.

As always, one of the most helpful things you

can do is to universalize the practice, to expand your view to include the suffering of the entire human race. Pain and the fear of pain is not yours alone or that of another single person. If you understand this deeply, it releases you from the private prison of pain and fear, and it is your shared connection to everyone on the planet.

feeling emotionally numb

Some people have the opposite problem. Instead of feeling overwhelmed by emotions, they feel completely numb when they try to do tonglen. Even if their minds were churning with emotions during sitting meditation, as soon as tonglen begins they blank out. They have no feelings at all and can't connect with their heart.

This was my experience when I first practiced tonglen. I would go totally numb as soon as the bell rang to signal tonglen. When it rang again to signal the end, I would wake up with a start, and had no idea what I had been doing for the past fifteen minutes. What really changed the practice for me was doing it during my daily life. This is the practice that I call "tonglen on the spot." Whenever I would see something in my daily life that was heartbreaking and I felt powerless to help, I would do tonglen. I also did it whenever I felt uptight, especially when I felt stuck in a relationship. I discovered that tonglen would open up the space between me and the other person. After doing this on-the-spot practice, I no longer felt numb during formal tonglen. My heart was accessible and I had endless material to work with. This is why I recommend tonglen on the spot so highly. Once you click into the tonglen attitude in daily life, it becomes much more real on the cushion.

fear of being polluted

Some people fear that they will be polluted and become sick by breathing in other people's pain and sickness, and so they shut down to protect themselves. When they breathe in, they imagine that they are a big sack that is being filled up with poison. But this is a fundamental misunderstanding of the practice. When we breathe in, we are aspiring to relieve another person of their suffering, but we're not actually taking in their AIDS virus or clinical depression or rage. Perhaps very advanced meditators, like the Buddha and *Milarepa*, could actually take on another person's sickness, but that is not what we're trying to do in the practice.

In his excellent book, *The Tibetan Book of Living and Dying*, Sogyal Rinpoche gives a method of practicing tonglen that helps to understand it properly. When you're breathing in what is unwanted or difficult—whether the pain and confusion of another person or your own unwanted feelings—you could imagine it as a strong darkness that dissolves the hard armor surrounding your heart. Here, the armor is an image for the solidification of ego. The heart is armored against any pain or unwanted feelings. It has been covered over by a shell, tightly constricted and unable to breathe. But the true nature of the heart is like the sun, which continuously shines but just happens to be covered by clouds. Breathing in the darkness dissolves the thickness of the cloud formations. Then the sun of maitri and compassion can shine forth without any barrier.

When you breathe in darkness, rather than feeling that it is a harmful poison or contamination, you can think of it as a very healing force. It dissolves the barriers that cause us suffering and confusion. In that way, it unlocks the heart's openness and tenderness, which is experienced as cool and healing, fresh and light. If you think of it in this way, the heart is opening all the time, both on the inbreath and outbreath. First it opens as we breathe in and dissolve the barriers, then it opens even further as we breathe out.

You can use other images to counteract the feeling that you are taking in more than you can handle. As you breathe in, you could think that your heart expands infinitely to accommodate whatever enters it. Or you could imagine your body as a hollow container, not made of solid flesh and bones, or a transparent hologram made out of space and light.

not knowing what to send out

Some people are stumped when they try to send out something healing on the outbreath. Either they send out something so vague and general that it ceases to be meaningful or, when they try to get more specific, they get conceptually tangled up in trying to find an exact remedy for a particular problem. Or perhaps they can't think of anything at all.

It's fine to experiment with different approaches. The most important point is that it feels real to you. For some people, the word "kindness" or "compassion" genuinely resonates, but for many it is too abstract—it's just an empty word. Some people like to send out vast space, like the ocean or the sky, in order to contact the freedom of a bigger perspective. Some people prefer an awe-inspiring natural image like the Grand Canyon or the snow-capped peaks of the Himalayas. Some people just send out a sense of relaxing or a big sigh of relief.

Some people like to send something very con-crete—a warm hug, a beautiful spring day, or a good meal—to a particular person. This gesture of giving feels much more real to them than the idea of compassion, which seems too theoretical. If you're this kind of person, you can begin to take notice of experiences that cheer up your daily life and make you grateful for the goodness of being alive. Then later, when it's time to send out some-thing with the outbreath, you'll have a better sense of what would be good to send.

As an example, I have a friend who wanted to do tonglen to work with a very difficult relation-ship with her schizophrenic father. But she couldn't come up with anything genuine to send him; everything seem contrived. She didn't have a clue what her father needed and even felt it was presumptuous to think that she did. But one day she just got the idea of sending him a good cup of coffee, and she could imagine him receiving it and smiling. So it worked.

As another example, one woman who came to Gampo Abbey for a lojong retreat had suffered severe sexual abuse from her father. She told me that she strongly identified with caged birds; she herself felt like a bird in a cage. So during tonglen she would take in all the caged birds on the inbreath; on the outbreath, she would open the door and let all the birds out. One day as she was doing this exchange, she had an image that all the birds flew out and one bird landed on a man's shoulder. When the man turned around, it was her father. That was a real breakthrough for her, and she experienced a moment of forgiveness.

When it comes down to it, we never actually know what someone else is experiencing. It seems to us that someone seems to be stuck or is having a hard time, but we can't be sure. So we don't even have to give a conceptual label to what we send to them. Personally, I think that the less you name what comes in and goes out, the better.

Sometimes it is a matter of simply breathing in and out with the intention of healing the situation for ourselves and others, without any specific idea of what the remedy is. Just staying with the breath and creating some space is good enough. That slows everything down so that we're able to connect with it in a nonverbal way. So the breath is just a way of staying with the shared humanness of the experience.

GETTING FURTHER SUPPORT

When you are practicing tonglen, it is highly recommended that you find a meditation instructor who you can work with. Especially in the beginning, you will have a lot of questions about the practice that may not be addressed in this book. And when you come up against obstacles, it is good to have someone to talk to. At the end of this book is a list of Shambhala Centers, where tonglen is regularly practiced. By contacting one of these centers, you should be able to find a meditation instructor who has experience in doing tonglen.

A community of fellow practitioners, or sangha, can be a wonderful support for your personal practice. It is very nurturing to share your experiences with other people. To your surprise, you will probably discover that they have the same kinds of questions and problems that you do. Even if they are not experts in the practice, often it is enough just to express what you are experiencing and get some friendly feedback.

You might want to join or start a tonglen/ lojong study group. People could meet, for example, once a month to practice sitting and tonglen for an hour, then study the teachings. The format doesn't really matter. You could read from a book on lojong teachings or listen to a tape, then have a discussion.

If you are working with deep-seated personal issues, such as addiction and abuse, you may need to do something in addition to practicing meditation. You may need to seek therapy. This might take the form of joining a support group like AA or Al-Anon. Or it might be working one-on-one with a therapist, preferably someone who is trained in meditation and understands the principles of bodhichitta practice.

am often asked the question, "Does tonglen really help the people I am doing it for?" I think that it does. First of all, tonglen definitely benefits each of us because our hearts and minds become more open; it awakens our bodhichitta or good heart. It can also help other people, although the results may not be immediately obvious — and it certainly can't harm them. It is difficult to explain how this works; it's somewhat magical. It obviously doesn't work as a direct cause and effect relationship: I do tonglen for you, therefore you get well. But some kind of energy is being worked with in the greater environment.

Trungpa Rinpoche has said that people become sick because there is a problem with their environment, because they feel so cramped and claustrophobic. Tonglen is a gesture that creates more openness, so that others can feel more space and relaxation and ease in their lives. So it creates a healthier atmosphere for everyone, ourselves and others.

Dr. Larry Dossey has written books on the effects of prayer on healing, including *Healing Words: The Power of Prayer and the Practice of Medicine*. He reports that prayer on behalf of others has a positive effect on their health. It has even been documented that prayer effects the growth rate of bacteria and fungi! One study showed that cardiology patients healed fifty to one-hundred percent more quickly when people prayed for them. So there seems to be some greater energy field through which we can communicate our caring for others.

The effectiveness of the practice depends on the fact that all of us are interconnected, which Thich Nhat Hanh calls "interbeing." There is a fine-tuned ecology between each of us, and each of our actions has a wide effect, just like ripples from dropping a pebble in a pond. Each time we open and help someone, it has a ripple effect. Instead of adding more fear, aggression, and paranoia in the world, we're adding more nonaggression, openness, and loving-kindness. As individuals are transformed at an inner level, the benefit spreads to their families, to their communities, and to the world.

It's like breaking the four-minute mile. When one person finally does it, many other people find out that, somewhat mysteriously, they are also able to do it. In the same way, when one person is willing to think of other people first, it enables more and more people to tap into bodhichitta. It changes something in the atmosphere so that the whole planet can be transformed.

In my own experience, when I do tonglen for someone who is in a desperate situation, such as a homeless person living on the street, I find that I'm no longer intimidated by them. Then I can look in their eyes, talk to them, and connect with them as fellow human beings. This in itself is very beneficial. People living on the street say that the most painful thing for them — more painful than the fact that they don't have a home or money — is that people rush by without looking in their eyes or acknowledging their existence. What they want the most is to be acknowledged as human beings. People in hospitals have the same kind of experience. So if tonglen enables us to connect with a fellow human being, I think that's definitely a benefit.

I have found that, when I do tonglen for a painful relationship, it seems to benefit the other person as well as myself. Even if I can't do the practice explicitly for the other person because I'm feeling so uptight toward them, it still seems to benefit them by changing the chemistry of the relationship.

There are many stories about the positive effects of tonglen for people who are dying. Even if they don't realize that someone else is doing tonglen for them, they will open their eyes and say, "I don't know what you're doing, but keep doing it." They feel less cramped and claustrophobic and a greater sense of space, of room to relax.

In conclusion, I like Trungpa Rinpoche's reply to the question if tonglen really works: When someone at the other end of the earth is hurting, wouldn't it help them to know that somebody cared? You see, it's not all that metaphysical; it's simple and very human.

This chapter contains questions about tonglen that have been asked during the many seminars that I have given on the practice. For convenience, they have been collected here under three different headings:

General questions

Questions about technique

Tonglen for real-life situations

GENERAL QUESTIONS

You have said that tonglen is a practice of transformation. What's the difference between transformation and trying to change yourself?

There is a very important distinction between transformation and change. Change implies struggling against something, but transformation does not occur through struggle. Somehow we have been programmed to feel that (1) there is something wrong with us and (2) we need to fix it. We feel that we need to change ourselves and become better people. We need to get rid of our ugly qualities: anger, jealousy, addiction, and all the rest. But this is an extremely aggressive and harmful way to think about ourselves. By contrast, our view is that sentient beings are basically good and complete just as they are and that meditation practice allows transformation to occur by itself, without trying to change something.

You might ask, "Does that mean I can never change—that I have to suffer, for example, from addictive behavior for the rest of my life?" Well, that's a very reasonable question. I believe that, if your logic is based on trying to change yourself, nothing will actually change, except perhaps temporarily. Such an approach cannot work in the long run, because it fights against our basic energy, whereas transformation is honoring our inherent energy as the source of wisdom and compassion.

Ironically, transformation doesn't happen by trying to change things. It comes only by seeing clearly. If you see clearly enough, you begin to see through the barriers of ego-clinging. You can't get rid of ego by taking it into the middle of the Atlantic Ocean, attaching an anchor to it, and dropping it to the bottom of the sea. That's because ego isn't a thing. It's a conglomeration of patterns and habits that have no substance at all as soon as you look into them deeply. Nevertheless, those patterns and habits have completely convinced us that they are real, and they motivate everything we do. The trick is to look at them again and again, with as much clarity and maitri as you can. Then, when you begin to see through them, they no longer have a hold on you. Then that's real transformation.

Does tonglen make us accept suffering in the world, so that we don't care about changing it?

Tonglen is not about accepting injustice and cruelty, but it is also not about righteous indignation. It is about a fundamental, true change. It is based on understanding that compassion is a relationship between equals, rather than some kind of pity or martyrdom. It involves touching in with the truth of your own experience, rather than shutting down to it, and then being able to open to others. In this way, when other people trigger a feeling like aggression in you, you aren't afraid of it. Or maybe you are still afraid of the feeling, but you work with it in a gentle, self-compassionate way.

Tonglen is the basis for compassionate communication. Instead of trying to overcome social injustice with a sense that you are attacking an enemy, you begin to stand in another person's shoes and understand how people see things very differently. Then, instead of a situation being frozen and blocked, it can evolve. Real communication can take place and real change can happen. But it starts at a very personal level: acknowledging your own situation, breathing in and opening your heart to what you're feeling, and then acknowledging that others also feel it.

In developing compassion, how can I work with limitations, such as my financial and energy resources?

What's the difference between setting reasonable limits and holding onto ego?

On the bodhisattva path, generosity is described as giving with a completely open heart and mind. At the inner level, there's no limit on how wide we can open our hearts. However, at the outer level, we do have a limited amount of energy and resources. So we have to go at our own pace.

This is like the analogy of bodhisattvas inviting all beings as their guests. At first, you may not be ready to open your door to the entire world. So you open your door just a little bit, but with the aspiration to open it all the way eventually. You open it at your own pace and sometimes you have to close it. But you don't close it forever. You get to know the nature of your fear and become more brave. By being honest and gentle with yourself, you become much more skillful in working with your own energy.

How can I know the difference between genuine compassion and idiot compassion?

Idiot compassion means always trying to please someone and giving them whatever they want, even if it's not really good for them. You're always nice, always comforting, always smiling. But you never say, "No, that's not okay." You don't set boundaries, which is what might really be needed.

For example, if someone is being aggressive and harming the environment, idiot compassion is to try to be conciliatory and very kind instead of just saying no. This approach is based on fear that the person might not like you or you might provoke a painful confrontation, or maybe you're just too tired to take a stand. Of course, if your child were just about to put her hand on the stove, you would never say, "That's okay, honey. Go ahead." You would yell "Stop!" at the top of your lungs. Such genuine compassion might seem harsh at times. But idiot compassion is not compassion at all; it is more like self-indulgence.

As our practice of compassion matures, we know better what will help someone else by knowing what really helps ourselves. We grow in both wisdom and skillful means: the knowledge of what needs to be done and the ability to do it. Wisdom often develops before skillful means: we understand what's needed but we still can't act on it. But over the years we learn from our mistakes, and our skillfulness comes into balance with our wisdom.

*If pain is such a good teacher, why should I wish
for myself and others to be rid of it?*

Some people have told me, "Almost everything I've
learned comes from pain, and seeking happiness
has only brought me trouble." It's true, we do learn
from pain. Working with it is the key to transforming our deepest habitual patterns. But when we
breathe in with the wish for people to be free of
pain, actually we are wishing for them not to have
to struggle, not to harden, not to shut down whenever they contact pain. We are also wishing that we
all could be softened by our pain, rather than let it
escalate into the kind of words and actions that
only make matters worse. Tonglen is a perfect example of how we can use pain to discover our capacity for love and caring and real joy in sharing
our lives with others, instead of its always trigger-
ing our aggression and making our hearts harder.

*Is it really possible to dissolve all boundaries? If I
open my heart completely, perhaps people will
walk all over me.*

We're not talking about doing away with all boundaries. The essence of the practice is being there

for another person, based on having unlimited compassion for yourself. If you can be steadfast with yourself—without wincing, without shutting down, without condemning, without judging—you can be there for others.

Setting boundaries is actually compassionate, both for yourself and others. The barriers of ego cause confusion and escalate suffering. But setting good boundaries creates clarity and allows for communication to happen. For example, suppose you are stuck in a relationship where you are beaten. The question is, why do you to allow this to happen to yourself again and again? It's a complicated situation, but it involves some kind of ignorance. You are not willing to look into what's going on. You blindly hope that somehow happiness will come from staying in a relationship that's fundamentally destructive. But at some point—usually with the help of other people and through strengthening your reservoir of courage, clarity, and self-compassion—you are able to say: "If you hit me one more time, I'm out of here."

Of course, setting boundaries takes a lot of courage. The other person—your spouse, your boss, your child—will probably get angry and not want to hear it. But at least they will know where they stand. So whether you say, "This doesn't work for me, I'm leaving," or you decide to stay and work with the situation, at least there is clarity.

We say that the practice of tonglen dissolves the barriers of ego, but this does not mean we cannot have boundaries. Our egos want everything on their own terms because of fear: fear of groundlessness, fear of openness, fear of being out of control. Through the practice of facing our fear and becoming more open, barriers of ego dissolve and confidence in our basic goodness and dignity as human beings grows. Then, out of respect for ourselves and others, we can create clear boundaries, because we have more insight into what is conducive to sanity and genuine caring.

When we dissolve ego's barriers with tonglen, it's not as if we were punishing ourselves, slapping ourselves silly. In fact, we become much clearer. A very important aspect of bodhichitta is *prajna*, or intelligence. Prajna sees through any tendency to build up our ego, which is based on fear and struggle. In this way, it provides space to relax, soften, and be more at home in our world. So instead of becoming more disabled through this process, we become more fully human and more able to live and die without fear.

If suffering is like a dream or an illusion, what is the purpose of doing tonglen?

There is more to the Buddhist view of reality than the slogan, "Regard all dharmas as dreams." That's just one side of it. To be more accurate, the Buddhist view is that you can't pin down what's happening. Although you try to make the world solid and secure with your mind, you never know for sure the true state of affairs. Whether we label our experience as good or bad, right or wrong, real or unreal, we are trying to gain some kind of reality check or confirmation of our identity. On the one hand, we can't just say, "Everything is solid and monolithic." On the other hand, we can't just say, "Everything is empty; pain is just an illusion." Both statements fall short of the truth.

The real Buddhist view is openness that goes beyond yes and no, solid and not solid, dream and not a dream. It is an open mind and heart that doesn't fixate on theories or beliefs. So the purpose of the practice is to loosen up the kind of thinking that makes things concrete and dependable and to relax into fundamental groundlessness and warmth.

What can I do during tonglen when I feel guilty about my relatively insignificant sufferings? They seem so disproportionate to the terrible sufferings of some people.

I don't think your sufferings are insignificant. Of course, someone might be in more physical pain or have a more desperate life situation than you do. But your feelings of guilt—not to mention your loneliness, your anger, your jealousy, your sadness, or your feelings of inadequacy—are as unwanted and painful as those of others. You don't need to make a big deal out of your feelings, but remember that they are the way for you to empathize with other people's suffering. You can't stand in another person's shoes until you stand completely in your own.

Our idea of compassion for others is sometimes mixed with feelings of our own unworthiness. As children, we were raised to think that we should put others before ourselves, which only fed into the belief that we weren't good enough. Tonglen is a chance to turn that around, to realize that genuine love and compassion for others is always based on love and compassion for yourself. You and others are linked inseparably. When you do tonglen, you are always doing it for yourself and others simultaneously. So you can send maitri and compassion to yourself and to all the other people who feel guilty about loving themselves. And if it helps, you could think of sending love to yourself as a child.

People often feel guilty if they think their life is easier than others'. But it would be just as reasonable to feel gratitude for having a good life right now. You never know what kind of suffering you might have to face in the future: you might have a stroke or find out that you have cancer, or your child might be killed in an accident. Of course, there's no point in fearing the worst. But if you think about the possibility of losing what you cherish, it could heighten your sense of gratitude and the preciousness of life.

What can I do when I find it difficult to do tonglen for myself, because it's so hard to stay with my own pain?

Of course, it is very common to feel overwhelmed. Many people find that they have to do it backwards and start with other people's pain. For example, if you are very fearful, it might be easier to start by doing tonglen for your friend's fear and then expanding it to yourself. You can use whatever works, but definitely don't use the practice to skip over your own feelings.

I like to call this practice the "great exposé," because it shows you all the ways you usually try to hide. When you do everything for others so that you don't have to feel your own pain, that's not called compassion—it's called martyrdom. So it's fine to begin with other people's pain, but be sure to include yourself at some point. At whichever end you begin, the practice always includes both self and other. Over time, you will realize the profound truth of the practice: the sameness or interconnectedness of self and other. The best remedy for feeling overwhelmed is to identify and empathize with others.

QUESTIONS ABOUT TECHNIQUE

What can I do if I have difficulty with breathing during tonglen?

This is a fairly common problem. It's one of the reasons that I recommend doing tonglen on the spot. In daily life, when things seem to be closing in on you, you can take the attitude that you are willing to be present and open to whatever is happening. It is irrelevant whether you are breathing in or out; you are simply present. Then, breathing in is opening and sending out is also opening.

In the formal practice, you may get the feeling that your throat is tightening or closing down as you breathe. When that happens, it's good to remember that breathing is not the main point of the practice—it's just a tool for staying with the present moment. So you could relax and shift your focus away from your throat and the physical process of breathing. You can imagine that you are breathing in and out from all the pores of your body or from a very large heart.

Whenever breathing seems to be a problem, you could just acknowledge that fact and realize that many other people also experience it. You can also exaggerate the breathing somewhat: breathe in deeply and breathe out equally deeply. It is helpful to consider both breathing in and breathing out as a process of opening. Then you don't have to keep track of which is in and which is out.

It helps to acknowledge the panic and then open your whole being. Imagine that you become the sky and just open to it, so there's really no place for it to get stuck. You are reversing a tendency to clutch and close down by tightening your throat and your belly and your whole being. As you breathe in, you can physically relax and then send out that relaxation.

When I breathe in the textures of dark, hot, and heavy, where do they go?

This is a very common question. When Trungpa Rinpoche first presented tonglen, some students had a "black bag theory." The theory was that you breathed into a big sack that stored all the poisonous stuff—which was, of course, a complete misunderstanding. One student said at the time, "I do the practice, but secretly I hope that it doesn't work."

Trungpa Rinpoche described the process of tonglen as a form of spiritual ecology. It is like sitting in a room so filled with dark coal dust that nobody can see. During tonglen, everyone breathes in the hot coal dust and sends out fresh cool light, so that eventually the air in the room is completely clean.

We could try to use the philosophical teachings

on emptiness and say that both yourself and what you breathe in aren't really substantial; they aren't really all that solid. But when you're up against a really difficult situation, philosophy isn't very helpful. So I prefer to use the image of the heart opening up wide: the pain and darkness enter a gigantic space inside your heart that can absorb any amount of pollution.

The darkness we breathe in is really only a visualization that we create in our minds. It represents the tendency of our hearts and minds to shut down and harden. It isn't some thing that we could get rid of, for example, by locking it in a box and throwing it over a cliff. It isn't something foreign that we are taking into our system. We're just learning to open. We open on the inbreath by taking the darkness into a vast open heart. We open on the outbreath by sending out spaciousness and light. Either way, in or out, we are opening further and further.

When I breathe out the textures of cool, white, and light, where do they come from?

In one of Sogyal Rinpoche's variations on the technique, black light comes in and dissolves the barriers around the heart so that the self-existing white light inside can radiate out. You could say that the white light is bodhichitta, which is always present, although we generally don't experience it because it's armored and closed off. So breathing in the black light dissolves the fixation and grasping that obscure the natural state. Then you can automatically send out the white light of bodhichitta.

This understanding of the practice is very profound. Just like the air you breathe, bodhichitta doesn't belong to you or to anyone. It is an always present and self-existing richness that you can tune into it at any time. As you tune into it more and more, you have more and more to give.

Do I always have to go through all four stages of the practice during a session?

When you do tonglen on the spot, you definitely don't need to go through all the stages. You go directly to stage three, taking in the pain that you see in the environment or that you are feeling yourself, then sending out relief to yourself and others.

When you begin doing the formal tonglen

technique, it is helpful to learn it thoroughly by going through all the stages step-by-step. Later, when you feel at home with the practice, you could spend less time on the second stage, which seems too conceptual for some people. If it really doesn't work for you, you could omit it altogether. There is a lot of room for making the practice your own. However, I think it's always important to do the fourth step of expanding the practice to others.

What can I do if the fourth stage of extending to others seems very abstract and theoretical to me?

Of course, a sense of realness in the practice is very important. When you try to think of "people in the same boat," maybe it doesn't feel very real; it seems a little too theoretical. But even if it doesn't seem very real to you, doing the fourth phase is very important, because it will begin to stretch and expand the world as you now experience it. The key to making the whole thing more real is first getting in touch with whatever empathy and love you already feel. Once you touch a genuine feeling of compassion, for the most part the stretching begins to happen by itself. But first you have to keep reminding yourself that there's a bigger world out there.

What if I can't coordinate the in- and outbreaths with the visualizations of sending and taking? Sometimes I feel that I need five minutes for each exchange.

If you contact something that touches you very deeply, it may become difficult to synchronize it with one inbreath and one outbreath. That is why I advocate doing tonglen on the spot. The more immediate and real things are, the easier it is to do it. If you do tonglen on the spot in your daily life — as you're walking down the street, sitting in a traffic jam, waiting in a long line at the market, or whatever painful situation presents itself — coordination with the in- and outbreath seems to work naturally. Once you are familiar with doing tonglen on the spot, you won't get bogged down when you do it on the cushion.

Sometimes people ask if they can spend, for example, three complete breaths with the sense of taking in and three complete breaths with the

sense of sending out. I usually tell them it's fine to
do it that way. After all, no one is watching!

Sometimes when I do the practice, I try to contact the fearful or painful feeling without worrying about the in- or outbreath. I just stay with the
feeling, giving it a lot of space as I breathe in and
giving it a lot of space as I breathe out. This
method can help you get over the concept that the
emotion on the outbreath has to be completely
different than the emotion on the inbreath.

*In group practice, can I continue practicing
tonglen after the bell has rung?*

Yes, it is fine to continue doing tonglen for as long
as you like. But it is definitely a good idea to end
with some sitting practice. Sitting meditation has
the quality of the first flash of absolute
bodhichitta. By repeatedly letting go of thoughts
and opening at the end of the outbreath, it connects you with a sense of bigger space and the
dreamlike nature of thoughts. For that reason, it is
always recommended to sandwich tonglen between two sessions of sitting meditation.

TONGLEN FOR REAL-LIFE SITUATIONS

At what point do we take action and actually try to help someone?

Needless to say, we try to benefit others with our words and deeds whenever possible. These days, the topic of engaged Buddhism has become popular in books and magazines. Thich Nhat Hanh and Joanna Macy are two major spokespersons for taking our practice of mindfulness and loving-kindness into the world.

There are many ways we can reach out to other people, and it doesn't have to be particularly dramatic. In the beginning it has to start close to home. It could be listening to a friend who is having a hard time and giving her a hug. It could be smiling at a person on the street and giving them some change. It could be working in a soup kitchen, doing hospice work, or helping with an important political campaign. Or it could be sharing a book on bodhichitta practice with someone you know is ready to hear these teachings.

Sometimes helping others might involve putting our own safety on the line. One man told me about being in his kitchen early in the morning and hearing a woman screaming in the street. He realized that, although he was willing to practice tonglen for her, he was quite happy to be safe in the kitchen and not outside. Finally, he and his housemates actually did go outside and help the woman. From this experience, he learned what it feels like to want to help but to hold back out of fear. He could empathize with the woman on the street and also with the people who didn't come outside to help.

This is a real-life situation that we could find ourselves in. It is interesting to ask ourselves what we would do. Obviously, we know that we should help, but shoulds and shouldn'ts don't get us very far in real life. We can't say for sure how we would react. We just don't know. Such self-honesty is humbling. If we are honest about how we feel and where we stand in our present stage of personal growth, we won't end up condemning other people.

Courage is not only running into the street to help. It is courageous to dedicate the rest of your life to opening your heart. It is also courageous to be honest about where you stand right now and to experience the groundlessness of not knowing what you would do.

How can I practice tonglen in difficult situations?
Tonglen on the cushion is fine, but when I go to
the office I still react to situations that provoke my
anger.

Tonglen is somewhat the Buddhist equivalent of
counting to ten. You go into the situation at the
office—and there it is, the anger and the aggression. Your only guideline is to practice one day at a
time, or one breath at a time, to the best of your
ability. You can make the aspiration, "Starting right
now and for the rest of my life, I'm going to explore what it means not to repress and not to act
out my anger." This is what Buddhists call the
"middle way," which is the path of avoiding extremes. Having made such an aspiration, you also
allow yourself to fail, knowing that you can learn a
lot from your mistakes.

Right in the middle of a conflict, you breathe in
and contact whatever is being provoked in you and
send out a sense of spaciousness into the environment. You breathe in with the recognition that many
people working in offices are feeling what you feel.
You realize that this feeling is both universal and
personal at the same time. This is particularly useful,
for example, when someone is actually yelling at you.

Then, of course, you have to respond. You can't just stand there, breathing in and out for the whole day. You're probably worried that the first word out of your mouth will just add to the aggression. Instead of reacting immediately, you breathe in and out for as long as you need to, with the idea of fully owning your feelings. After that, you just trust what comes out of your mouth. It will probably be a lot different than what you would have said if you were trying to resolve the situation by speaking out harshly or by repressing your feelings.

In tonglen you're not trying to resolve anything. You're just trying to be with the pain completely, to soften around it, and to see what happens. It's not about chilling out; it's about fully being there. This is not conflict resolution — in fact, there may be no final resolution. It's more like transforming the core of your being by opening your heart and mind to the situation.

In the lojong teachings, this is called the "transformation of bad circumstances into the path of enlightenment." It is not called the "eradication of bad circumstances" so that our lives will be hunky-dory forever and ever. Life is both cruel and kind, hideous and exquisite. Tonglen is training in staying open to all aspects of our lives.

You definitely have to go at your own speed, very gently and patiently. Opening your heart to difficult and dangerous situations does not happen over-night—it's a lifetime journey. If tonglen at the office is too difficult because you feel so vulnerable and unsafe, then try working with it in easier situations. Later, when you get in the habit of opening your heart and mind, you will find that you can do it wherever you are. Ultimately, the practice will give you confidence in your own strength—and that's the kind of safety you need.

How can I use tonglen to work with addiction?

It's the same way we work with aggression. We stay with it and stay with it, and we still may find ourselves screaming at someone. When we work with a lot of self-honesty and self-compassion, we get in touch with our addictions, which contain so much heavy-duty ignoring. We come to know our addictions very well, but that doesn't mean we no longer act on them.

My personal addictions have not been as crippling as, for example, heroin addiction. But I have spent years working with very strong habitual patterns. So I understand what it's like to be unable to break them, and I have great empathy for all the other people who can't stop.

First we have to get at the root of the addiction. In addition to doing tonglen and developing self-compassion, this process may include a lot of other psychological work. I think that my addictions have started to unwind by getting to know the chain reaction of suffering that comes from fulfilling them. In the moment, the promise of relief seems just as strong, but some reservoir of intelligence begins to click in. You say to yourself, "Wait a minute! Haven't I done this before? Has it ever brought me anything but a momentary gratification and then terrible regret?"

So how do you sow the seeds of your inner strength? It's by staying with the irritation and restless energy with gentleness, compassion, and honesty. And when you find yourself saying, "I can't," you understand completely why other people can't and you feel empathy for them.

Linda Jones, a friend and student of mine, has written a book that I would recommend. It is about working with addiction and abuse issues by using tonglen and the lojong slogans. It's called *The Little Handbook for Trauma Survivors*. This is not a love-and-lighty practice for people who already have it all together. It is very relevant to the nitty-gritty, heavy-duty challenges that we deal with in our lives.

How can I do tonglen for an abusive relationship?

First of all, if you're in an abusive relationship, you need to do more than practice tonglen. You probably need to get out of it. Of course, that's easier said than done. First you need to take care of yourself at the outer level, for example, by moving to a place where you're safe. Then you can begin to work with it at the inner level. If you're in the middle of a situation where you're really being hurt, it's unrealistic to think that you can solve it merely at the inner level.

You may discover that your current relationship is part of an old pattern you have been repeating for years. From a friend who is a social worker, I heard the story of a nineteen-year-old woman who was in an abusive relationship with her current lover and had previously been in one with another man. My friend helped to remove her from her situation and to place her in a safe and caring environment in a different city. But tragically, within four months, she was in another abusive relationship.

The lesson of this story is that we have to work

with the relationship on an inner level, or else it will continue to manifest on the outer level. Tonglen is one powerful way to work with it. But any way you can work with it on the inner level is important, because our old habits are a major part of the problem. Even when we understand this, it is still very hard to change old habits.

To undo the knot of self-destruction at its core, I recommend the approach of welcoming feelings associated with the old habits and developing an attitude of gentleness and honesty with yourself. Sitting meditation and tonglen can be enormously supportive in this process. But, generally speaking, you also need someone that you can work with regularly, like a therapist, because you need a lot of support to get through difficult abusive patterns.

How can I practice tonglen for someone who abuses his wife? I can appreciate that he is a fellow human being, but I can't overlook what he's done.

Of course not. Particularly if he's abused you or someone you love. I would not tell you, "You should forgive the abuser." That would be meaningless, because you are not ready to do that. At this point, just work with your genuine feeling of not being able to forgive. You don't have to be ashamed of that feeling.

I have worked with people who were tragically abused as children. I find that, when they are willing to open to the pain they feel and do tonglen for themselves and all the other children who have been abused, compassion and forgiveness evolves by itself. So just start where you are. Work with compassion for yourself and the people you love, then gradually expand it into more difficult areas, to people you couldn't possibly have compassion for right now. Let evolution take its course. But at the same time, don't try to live up to any "shoulds."

How can I do tonglen for an alcoholic, particularly when I feel that they are taking advantage of me?

I think you need to do more than just practice tonglen. It would be helpful for you to join a support group like Al-Anon. It would be an eye-opener for you to talk with other people who have alcoholic partners or parents. Then, within the group, you might feel comfortable sharing what you know about tonglen practice.

How can I work with sadness? It feels like tenderness mixed with a hint of despair.

Trungpa Rinpoche used to talk about the "genuine heart of sadness," which is the tenderness you're referring to. That's the virtue of sadness: it has tenderness in it, even when there is despair. It is a problem only when we don't stay with the sadness, but cover it with a hard protective shell.

A native American teacher told me she felt that this practice was about developing the strength and courage to touch the center of our pain and joy and finding the tenderness in it. It is about connecting with our inherent vulnerability or soft spot and learning to trust it, without masking it over with something hard or defensive like coldness or speediness. Touching into the soft spot is the magic for finding a sense of joy and well-being that doesn't depend on the weather of one's emotions.

How can I use tonglen to work with a serious illness? Recently diagnosed with cancer, I find myself alternating between hope and hopelessness.

In some hospices today, tonglen practice is introduced to terminally ill patients. They are instructed to breathe in with the wish that others could be free of the pain that they are feeling in the moment and to breathe out whatever might be helpful. This includes not only physical pain, but also the associated psychological suffering, such as shame, fear, rage, denial, depression, and loneliness. An AIDS patient once told me how he was working with this practice. At first, he was afraid and thought the practice would make his situation worse. But as he worked with it slowly over time, he was surprised to discover that being able to benefit other people gave meaning to his own pain and illness. The beauty of the practice is that it's not just about others and it's not just about self. It's really about our shared humanity.

If you have the courage, there is a revolutionary teaching that you could try to work with. It is expressed in a slogan:

If it's better for me to live, let me live.
If it's better for me to die, let me die.

This is similar to the attitude expressed in the lojong slogan, "Abandon any hope of fruition." Basically, it means that you surrender to not knowing what is best. You don't know whether you are going to live or die. You might die next week or in twenty years. But no matter how long you live, it is certain that you will experience less fear and regret at the moment of death if you have an attitude of opening and letting go than if you have an attitude of being completely shut down.

Letting go of hope is not fatalistic. Hope itself contains a lot of desperation and denial, so surrendering it is actually an opening. In this in-between time of uncertainty, you can do tonglen to make friends with the fear, the resistance, and the denial that surround your illness. Then you extend your practice to others.

For example, I wouldn't be surprised to hear that you have often woken up in the middle of the night. When you're lying there in the darkness, you could think about all the other people—young children, people your age, and elderly people—who are in a similar situation. Then you could do tonglen for people suffering with cancer or any other illness. This approach leads to having no regrets and being able to relax into groundlessness at the moment of death, whereas the approach of clutching onto life is like kicking and screaming at the edge of an abyss.

How can I use tonglen to work with intense physical pain?

Physical pain can be a great teacher. It can become a source of empathy for others if we learn how to universalize our experience. From the moment we notice pain, we begin to harden around it. And below the pain is the fear of "I'll never get better." From that hot point of pain and fear, we can go in either of two directions. We can go in the usual direction and become hardened and isolated, or we can soften and extend our caring to others.

The trick is to stay with the pain and fear, rather than dissociate from it, and to relax into it. So you practice letting go of your panicky thoughts and at the same time think of other people in the same situation—all with a very light touch. The most important thing is to be honest and kind: fully acknowledge what you're feeling and be kind to yourself. That is the only way to find the tenderness in the pain. Then, if you have the energy, also think, "My friend Mildred probably feels just like this" or "Many other people feel just like this." So you keep practicing in that way, and give up any hope of fruition.

I have personally worked with this a lot. For

many years I have suffered from chronic fatigue and have been bed-ridden for long stretches of time. Sometimes I have felt so weak that I couldn't breathe in pain even at the level of aspiration. I just couldn't handle it.

When you come to such an extreme point, the practice becomes more profound, because the physical pain forces you to get real. First you work with the experience of "I can't do it" and find the tenderness within that. Then you have a feeling of kinship with all the other people who can't do it. You think, "Our poor suffering bodies! Our poor fearful minds!"

Fortunately, there are drugs that can alleviate physical pain when it becomes more than we can bear. But I'm not talking so much about physical pain. I'm talking about working with all the mental suffering, the isolation and despair, that proliferates around it. This is where the real transformation can take place.

Is it helpful to do tonglen for a person who is dying or has recently died?

Yes. If you feel comfortable doing it, it is very helpful for yourself and the other person. You can just sit with them quietly and do tonglen. They don't even need to know that you are doing it. It may help take away their fear and allow them to relax into their death as a positive experience of return or opening, rather than as a terrifying experience.

After a person has died, in the Buddhist tradition it's encouraged that you stay with his or her body and practice tonglen. This is based on the belief that their consciousness remains for some time after death. Because they are still aware of their environment, tonglen helps to open up the space and allow for deep relaxation, lack of fear, and continuing with their spiritual journey. If the body doesn't have to be removed right away, it is good to sit with them and continue tonglen. After the body has been taken away, you can still continue to do tonglen for them, even though you're no longer in the same room.

This practice helps both yourself and the person who is dying or has died. For yourself, you feel that you're actually able to do something and you feel an especially intimate connection with him or her. Tonglen also helps the person who is dying. In the dying process, a person can get stuck in struggle and fear and not be able to let go. Tonglen allows the process to soften and open up, both for yourself and the person who is dying or has died.

In my experience, being with an ordinary person who is able to let go when dying is like being with an enlightened being. There is a very strong sense of spaciousness and freedom in the room as they dissolve back into vast space and timelessness. But for a person who can't let go, the experience is one of terror.

Should people do tonglen for themselves when they are dying?

Yes, this is definitely recommended. In *The Great Path of Awakening*, Jamgön Kongtrül says that doing tonglen is the best possible practice at the time of death. He says that you should meditate on maitri and compassion and practice tonglen, which is relative bodhichitta practice. He also says that you should rest your mind in the understanding that all your experiences of the world are dreamlike, which is absolute bodhichitta practice.

Of course, the most important thing is how you work with your life right now—not when you're just about to die. You never know. Tomorrow you might die suddenly in a car accident and not have the opportunity to practice. Now is the time to start training yourself in the tonglen attitude and in opening your mind.

In tonglen, how can I work with attachment to someone or something that I really like?

On the outbreath, you could send out the very thing you desire but without the attachment, the painful feeling of craving or addiction. Take chocolate, for example. With the inbreath, you could take in the chocolate with all the craving that goes with it; with the outbreath, you could send out the deliciousness of chocolate freed from its addictive quality. Or perhaps you need to change the scenario with the outbreath and to send out whatever feels completely open and spacious. Then, don't forget to take in everyone else's craving and to send them out enjoyment free from the pain of attachment.

What can I do if I feel physically ill from doing the practice?

Actually, it is not possible to get physically sick at our level of practice, which is the level of aspiration.

Very advanced meditators might literally be able to take on other people's sickness, but that is not what we're doing here. Of course, some people might feel a slight sense of illness, nausea, or headache while doing the practice or afterward. But this is a psychosomatic illness, based on our fear and resistance to the practice. In a sense, the feeling of illness is a reaction to groundlessness, because illness, although unpleasant, is something that you can get a hold on; it is tangible, graspable. In that way it confirms your existence.

the continuous practice of bodhichitta

The following is a summary of the various bodhichitta practices used for developing wisdom, maitri, and compassion in our lives. Not all the practices (for example, the *six paramitas*) are discussed in this book.

The following three noble principles can be applied to any practice you are doing:

In the beginning, start with the motivation of compassion.

In the middle, maintain a nongrasping attitude, free from the expectation of any results.

In the end, dedicate the merit of your practice for the benefit of all beings.

ABSOLUTE BODHICHITTA PRACTICE

Generally associated with awakening to the experience of shunyata, this practice introduces us to a
fluid, open way of thinking and to the unlimited
dimension of being. It is primarily a formal meditation practice based on shamatha-vipashyana (or
mindfulness-awareness). By clearly seeing the illu-
sory nature of thoughts and experience, things become flexible and workable. This essential openness is fundamentally inseparable from relative
bodhichitta practice.

RELATIVE BODHICHITTA PRACTICES

Generally associated with awakening compassion,
this practice introduces us to the open and unlimited capacity to love and care about each other.
There are two types: practices of aspiring and practices of entering.

practices of aspiring
    Practices for cultivating the four limitless ones:
maitri, compassion, joy, and equanimity. (See
"Maitri and Compassion Practices" on p. 119.)

The formal meditation practice of tonglen

Daily-life practice of relative bodhichitta:

> Making aspirations
> Equality practice
> Sharing your heart
> Tonglen on the spot
> Tonglen on the street

p r a c t i c e s   o f   e n t e r i n g
The daily life practices of the six paramitas, which lead us to the inseparable experience of shunyata and compassion: generosity, discipline, patience, exertion, meditation, and wisdom (Sanskrit: prajna). For a brief presentation of the paramitas, see Trungpa Rinpoche's books *Cutting Through Spiritual Materialism*, pp. 170–8; *The Myth of Freedom*, pp. 106–20; or *Meditation in Action*, pp. 35–74.

LOJONG PRACTICE

This is the practice of working with the slogans of mind training, also known as the slogans of Atisha, which include both absolute and relative bodhichitta practices. All fifty-nine slogans are discussed in Trungpa Rinpoche's *Training the Mind and Cultivating Loving-Kindness* and also in *Start Where You Are*.

Whenever you find that tonglen is too difficult, you could try doing the practices of maitri and compassion. On the outbreath, you simply send out the wish that yourself and others may enjoy happiness and be free from suffering. On the inbreath, you do not think that you are taking in others' suffering as in tonglen.

Maitri is summed up in the aspiration, "May all sentient beings enjoy happiness and the root of happiness." Compassion is summed up in the aspiration, "May they be free from suffering and the root of suffering." Here, the root of suffering is struggling to protect yourself from pain and shutting down the heart to the world. The root of happiness is giving up ego-clinging and giving birth to bodhichitta.

The maitri practice is done in seven stages. It begins by wishing happiness for yourself, then extending that wish step by step to others: someone to whom you feel very grateful, friends, neutrals, difficult people, all the above taken together, and finally all sentient beings.

The seven stages of compassion practice are identical to maitri practice, but the aspiration is slightly different. Instead of wishing simply for happiness, you wish for yourself and others to be free from physical and mental suffering.

MAITRI PRACTICE IN SEVEN STAGES

1 Send maitri to yourself. Think, "May I enjoy happiness and the root of happiness" or, more simply, "May I be truly happy." You can send to yourself something specific, like an act of kindness or trust that would make you happy, or you can just keep it general. It is completely appropriate to use you own words, so that the aspiration is meaningful to you.

2 Think of someone toward whom you feel sincerely grateful. Imagine that they are directly in front of you. Then send maitri to them. Think, "May he or she be happy." Again, use your own words to convey this and make it real to you.

3 In the same way, send maitri to a good friend or friends.

4 Send maitri to a neutral person or persons, someone you don't really know or feel indifferent toward.

5 Send maitri to a difficult person in your life.

6 Send maitri to everyone in steps one to five. Think, "May all of us enjoy happiness and the root of happiness." This stage is called "dissolving the barriers" between self and others.

7 Extend maitri toward all beings throughout the universe. Think, "May all beings without exception enjoy happiness and the root of happiness."

If you like, you can abbreviate the number of stages, but you should always begin with yourself and end with all beings.

GROUP PRACTICE

Tonglen is usually done during one session of sitting meditation in the course of a *nyinthün* or a *dathün*. If a group is meeting specifically to study and practice tonglen, an hour of sitting that includes tonglen could precede the class or discussion.

For group practice, a timekeeper signals the beginning and end of tonglen practice with a bell. Two quick rings begin tonglen and two *rolldowns* end it. Here is a possible schedule for a one-hour practice session:

Chant the Four Limitless Ones.
Sit for 30 minutes.
Practice tonglen for 10 minutes.
Sit for 20 minutes.
Chant the Dedications of Merit (see p. 127).

PRACTICE AT HOME

When you practice by yourself, be sure to do some sitting meditation both before and after tonglen. If you only have a short time to practice, it would probably be better just to sit. Here is a possible schedule for a one-hour practice session:

To begin, you could chant the Four Limitless Ones, Bodhisattva Vow, and/or Friendliness.
Sit for at least 15 minutes.
Practice tonglen for 10–15 minutes.
Sit for at least 10 minutes.
To end, you could chant the Dedications of Merit.

Although some people do not like to complicate their practice with chanting and ritual, others find that it is helpful and inspirational. In order to incorporate the three noble principles into your practice, you could begin a session with the Four Limitless Ones or the Bodhisattva Vow and end it with one or both of the Dedications of Merit. Friendliness is chanted during the Maitri Bhavana, but it could be used at any time.

FOUR LIMITLESS ONES

> May all sentient beings enjoy happiness and
>   the root of happiness.
> May they be free from suffering and the root of
>   suffering.
> May they not be separated from the great
>   happiness devoid of suffering.
> May they dwell in the great equanimity free
>   from passion, aggression, and prejudice.

BODHISATTVA VOW

> As earth and the other elements, together with
>   space,
> Eternally provide sustenance in many ways for
>   the countless sentient beings,
>
> So may I become sustenance in every way for
>   sentient beings
> To the limits of space, until all have attained
>   *nirvana.*
>
> As the *sugatas* of old gave birth to the
>   bodhichitta
> And progressively established themselves in the
>   training of a bodhisattva,

So I too, for the benefit of beings, shall give
    birth to the bodhichitta
And progressively train myself in that
    discipline.

—*Excerpted from* The Way of the
Bodhisattva, *Chapter Three*

ASPIRATIONS

All the virtue I have accomplished until this
    moment
And whatever I may accomplish in the future,
I dedicate for the welfare of all sentient beings.
Like a drop of water put into the ocean, may it
    never diminish.
May sickness, war, famine, and needless suffer-
    ing decrease.
May wisdom, love, and compassion increase
For myself and others, now and in the future.

—*Adapted from a Red Tara aspiration*

May the poor find wealth
And those oppressed by sorrow find joy.
May those who despair find hope
And those who are fearful discover fearlessness.
May the sick find health,
May the weak find strength,
And may all hearts join in friendship.
—*Adapted from* The Way of the
Bodhisattva, *Chapter Ten*

DEDICATIONS OF MERIT

By this merit, may all attain omniscience.
May it defeat the enemy, wrongdoing.
From the stormy waves of birth, old age,
sickness, and death,
From the ocean of *samsara*, may I free all
beings.

By the confidence of the golden *sun of the
great east*,
May the lotus garden of the *Rigden's* wisdom
bloom.
May the dark ignorance of sentient beings
be dispelled.
May all beings enjoy profound brilliant glory.

FRIENDLINESS

This is what should be done by those who are
   skilled in seeking the good, having attained
   the way of peace:

They should be able, straightforward, and
   upright, easy to speak to, gentle, and not
   proud,
Content and easily supported, with few
   obligations and wants,
With senses calmed, prudent, modest, and
   without greed for other people's possessions.
They should not do anything base that the wise
   would reprove.
May they be at their ease and secure—may all
   beings be happy.

Whatever living beings there are, whether they
   be weak or strong—omitting none—
Whether long, large, average, short, big or
   small,
Seen or unseen, dwelling near or far,
Born or to be born—may all beings be happy.

Let no one deceive another or despise anyone
   anywhere.

Let none out of anger or hostility wish suffering
upon another.

Just as a mother would protect with her life her
own child, her only child,

So should one cultivate a boundless mind
toward all beings and friendliness toward
the entire world.

One should cultivate a boundless mind—
above, below, and across,

Without obstruction, hatred, or enmity.

Standing, walking, sitting, or lying down,
throughout all one's waking hours,

One should practice this mindfulness;
this, they say, is the supreme state.

Not falling into wrong views, virtuous,
endowed with insight,

Having overcome desire for sense pleasures,
one will never again know rebirth.

Buddha Shakyamuni taught this Metta Sutta, *which is
found in the* Sutta-Nipata *section of the* Khuddaka-
Nikaya *collection of shorter-length discourses. It was
translated from the Pali by the Nalanda Translation
Committee with reference to a number of previous
translations.*

The Maitri Bhavana is a ceremony for the seriously ill that is a special application of tonglen practice. "Maitri" means friendliness or loving-kindness; "bhavana" means meditation or contemplation. It is usually done in a group, but you could do it individually for a relative or friend if you feel inspired to do so. When it is done in a group, everyone can do the practice, even people who have never done tonglen before.

Sometimes people feel that it might be dangerous to do this practice. They are afraid that they might literally take on other people's illnesses and become sick themselves. But this is a fundamental misunderstanding. When we do the practice for people who are sick, we do not think that we are actually breathing in their disease — their cancer or their AIDS. What we are breathing in is their tendency to shut down and become paralyzed by their physical pain, which is the real suffering. We breathe in with the wish to take away the suffering that surrounds their physical pain — despair, anger, resentment, denial, and feelings of isolation. Our aspiration is that their illness could be a genuine path of awakening for them, whether they recover or not.

Usually pain turns into fear and hardens us, making us more bitter and angry. But by learning to practice in this way, pain can soften us; it can make us gentler, more humble, more loving, and more grateful human beings. So this practice is not about curing; it's about healing. It's not really about getting rid of pain, which is an inherent part of human existence. It's about reconnecting with our true nature, the spaciousness of our hearts and minds.

PRACTICE LEADER'S INSTRUCTIONS

An announcement should be posted well in advance of the group practice, so that people can list the names and illnesses of their friends and relatives. Usually the leader is a senior practitioner and meditation instructor, but it is fine if a relative or friend of the sick person leads the ceremony, as long as they understand how to do it properly.

Sit for 10–20 minutes.

Ring the bell once and deaden it.

Announce: "We are going to do the practice of Maitri Bhavana, which means meditation on loving-kindness."

Read the "Commentary on Maitri Bhavana" by Trungpa Rinpoche.

Announce: "We will be doing this practice in particular for the following persons who are ill."

Read the list of names and illnesses.

Announce: "Next we will chant the text called Friendliness."

Ring the bell once and deaden it.

Chant Friendliness (see p. 128).

Announce: "Next we will do the practice of tonglen, or sending and taking."

Explain tonglen briefly in your own words.

Ring the bell two times briskly to begin tonglen.

Practice tonglen for 5–10 minutes.

End tonglen with two rolldowns and a full stop (medium-soft-loud) on the bell.

Sit for 10–20 minutes.

Chant the Dedications of Merit (see p. 127).

COMMENTARY ON MAITRI BHAVANA
by Chögyam Trungpa Rinpoche

In this practice we share health with other people—in fact, all sentient beings. It involves developing a sense of immense generosity and being willing to suffer for others. One's own personal gain and achievement could be shared—in fact, given up.

Generally sickness and unhealthiness occur from a problem with the environmental situation. People have no chance to express any sense of comfort because the space around them is so cramped. Consequently, one can get disordered in one's body and mind, and get sick because there is no accommodation to relax, open, and celebrate.

So this practice is a token or gesture to provide lots of room, openness, and space for others, and not make demands on the environment itself. In order to change the environment, one has to create some seed from within oneself. If one is creating one's own spaciousness, that spaciousness becomes contagious and expands to others who are suffering, so they also could be helpful. That seems to be the basic meaning of generosity in this practice.

The technique of meditation here is very old, and has come down through generations of *mahayana* practitioners. It is similar to working on the in- and outbreath, but is more like contemplation, in that deliberate thoughts, mental objects, are used. As you breathe out, you breathe out your spaciousness and your goodness completely. As you breathe in, you breathe into yourself the sickness, neurosis, and problems of other people. This is the practice that we are going to do.

GLOSSARY

Absolute Bodhichitta The basically open, ground-less, and ungraspable quality of all our experi-ence. It is very similar to the notion of shunyata.

Bodhichitta (Sanskrit: "mind/heart of awak-ening") Sometimes also called buddha nature, it is the awakened heart and mind inherent in all human beings. Bodhichitta is discussed in terms of absolute and relative bodhichitta, al-though these two aspects are inseparable.

Bodhisattva (Sanskrit: "warrior of awakening") A person who follows the path of cultivating bodhichitta, wisdom, and compassion in order to free all beings from suffering.

Bodhisattva Vow The vow to achieve complete awakening for oneself so that one can liberate all beings from suffering.

Dathün (Tibetan: "month sitting") A month-long meditation retreat that emphasizes shamatha-vipashyana. Tonglen practice is often introduced toward the end of the retreat. The retreat also in-cludes oryoki practice (Zen-style eating), taking the five Buddhist precepts, and periods of silence. Dathüns are regularly scheduled at Shambhala practice centers, such as Karmê Chöling, Rocky Mountain Shambhala Center, Dechen Chöling, Dorje Denma Ling, and Gampo Abbey.

Four Limitless Ones Four qualities that are cultivated by practitioners of the mahayana path: maitri, compassion, sympathetic joy, and equanimity (or equality).

Lojong (Tibetan: "mind training") A method of training the mind in reversing the habitual pattern of ego-clinging and developing maitri and compassion for oneself and others. These teachings by the Indian master Atisha (born 982 C.E.) were condensed into fifty-nine slogans under seven different headings, or points, by the Tibetan teacher Geshe Chekawa (1101–1175). Geshe Chekawa's text, along with a commentary by Jamgön Kongtrül Lodrö Thaye, are translated in *The Great Path of Awakening: A Commentary on the Mahayana Teaching of the Seven Points of Mind Training*. Trungpa Rinpoche's commentary on lojong is found in *Training the Mind and Cultivating Loving-Kindness*.

Lojong Slogans Fifty-nine guidelines, or sayings, used as a support for lojong practice. Lojong slogans are available in English in the form of cards, and even as a computer screen saver. Practitioners often keep a set of cards on their desk. By flipping over a new slogan each day, they are able to go through the entire set of slogans several times a year.

Mahayana (Sanskrit: "great vehicle") The great path of awakening, also called the "open path" or the "path of the bodhisattva." The mahayana path begins when one discovers bodhichitta in oneself and vows to develop it in order to benefit others. The path proceeds by cultivating absolute and relative bodhichitta. The result of the path is full awakening for the benefit of all beings. The mahayana is often compared with the hinayana ("lesser vehicle"), which focuses more on development of the individual.

Maitri (Pali: metta) Loving-kindness; unconditional friendliness toward oneself and others. It is the first of the four limitless ones.

Maitri Bhavana (Sanskrit: "meditation on loving-kindness") A tonglen practice specifically for people who are seriously ill.

Milarepa (1040-1123) One of Tibet's most renowned yogic practitioners and poets.

Nirvana (Sanskrit: "extinguished") Freedom from

the sufferings of samsara, or confused cyclic existence; complete awakening.

Nyinthün (Tibetan: "day sitting") A day-long meditation retreat, which includes the practices of shamatha-vipashyana and tonglen.

Prajna (Tibetan: sherap, "best knowing") Intelligence, knowledge; the natural clarity and sharpness of mind that sees and discriminates. At its most developed level, prajna can see directly—that is, in a way free from all concepts—the truths of impermanence, egolessness, suffering, and shunyata.

Relative Bodhichitta The basic human warmth that arises out of the openness of absolute bodhichitta. It contains the qualities of maitri and compassion.

Rigden A ruler of the enlightened kingdom of Shambhala, who represents the complete attainment of bravery and compassion.

Rolldown A rhythmic pattern played on a bell or drum that gradually accelerates and ends with three beats.

Samsara (Tibetan: khorwa, "spinning around") Confused existence; the world of struggle and suffering that is based on ego-clinging, conflicting emotions, and habitual patterns. Its root cause is ignorance of our true nature: openness beyond the duality of self and other.

Shamatha-vipashyana (Tibetan: shine-lhakthong, "dwelling in peace and seeing clearly") Also called sitting meditation, this is the most basic form of meditation in the Buddhist and Shambhala traditions. Instructions for the practice are found in all of Pema's books, for example, Chapter Four of *When Things Fall Apart*.

Shambhala International An association of meditation and practice centers founded by Trungpa Rinpoche in 1972; formerly known as Vajradhatu (Sanskrit: "indestructible space"). Shambhala Centers host programs in meditation, Buddhism, and the arts under the direction of Sakyong Mipham Rinpoche, who is Trungpa Rinpoche's son and successor.

Shantideva (c. 685-763) Author of *The Way of the Bodhisattva*, a key text on the mahayana path of developing the six paramitas.

Shunyata (Sanskrit: "emptiness") The open dimension of being; groundlessness; freedom from all conceptual frameworks. "Openness" is probably a better translation than "emptiness," since "emptiness" gives the mistaken impression that it is a completely blank state. In fact, it is a state insepa-

rable from compassion and all other awakened
qualities.

Six Paramitas (Sanskrit: "gone to the other
shore") Six qualities that are cultivated on the
path of a bodhisattva: generosity, discipline, patience, exertion, meditation, and wisdom
(prajna).

Six Points of Good Posture (1) Sitting squarely on
your seat, (2) legs crossed comfortably in front,
(3) upright but relaxed torso, (4) hands resting
palms down on the thighs, (5) eyes open with a
downward gaze, and (6) mouth slightly open.

Sugatas (Sanskrit: "well gone") Another name for
buddhas.

Sukhavati Ceremony Sukhavati is the Sanskrit name
of the pure land of Buddha Amitabha. The Sukhavati Ceremony is a Buddhist funeral ceremony
written by Trungpa Rinpoche. It includes practicing tonglen for the person who has died.

Sun of the Great East The Great Eastern Sun is an
important symbol in the Shambhala tradition,
representing indestructible wakefulness.

Tonglen (Tibetan: "sending and taking") The practice of exchanging oneself for others. In coordination with the in- and outbreaths, one thinks

that one takes on the pain and suffering of others and then sends them relief.

Trungpa Rinpoche The Venerable Chögyam Trungpa Rinpoche—meditation master, scholar, and artist—founded Naropa University in Boulder, Colorado; Shambhala Training; and Shambhala International. His books include *Cutting Through Spiritual Materialism, Shambhala: The Sacred Path of the Warrior,* and *Training the Mind and Cultivating Loving-Kindness.*

The Collected Works of Chögyam Trungpa, Volumes 1-8 (Shambhala: Boston and London, 2003) contain much of his published work. See www.shambhala.com for information on these and other books.

BIBLIOGRAPHY

Chödrön, Pema. *The Places That Scare You: A Guide to Fearlessness in Difficult Times.* Boston and London: Shambhala Publications, 2001.

Chödrön, Pema. *Start Where You Are: A Guide to Compassionate Living.* Boston and London: Shambhala Publications, 1994. A contemporary presentation of lojong training. Chapter One includes brief shamatha-vipashyana instruction; Chapter Six presents tonglen.

Chödrön, Pema. *When Things Fall Apart: Heart Advice for Difficult Times.* Boston and London: Shambhala Publications, 1997. Chapter Four presents shamatha-vipashyana instruction; Chapter Fifteen presents tonglen instruction.

Chödrön, Pema. *The Wisdom of No Escape and the Path of Loving-Kindness.* Boston and London: Shambhala Publications, 1991. Chapter Four presents shamatha-vipashyana instruction; Chapter Twelve presents tonglen instruction.

Druppa, Gyalwa Gendun. *Training the Mind in the Great Way.* Ithaca, NY: Snow Lion Publications,

1987. A traditional presentation of lojong training.

Jones, Linda B. *The Little Handbook of Trauma Survivorship: Lojong Slogans as a Path of Recovery*. This book by one of Pema's students presents lojong practice for people working with addiction and abuse issues. It can be ordered from the author: 25 Park Vale Avenue, Apt. 5, Allston, MA 02134, (617) 233-4135, Email: ljones@riversidecc.org

Khyentse Rinpoche, Dilgo. *Enlightened Courage*. Ithaca, NY: Snow Lion Publications, 1993. A traditional presentation of lojong training.

Kongtrül, Jamgön. *The Great Path of Awakening: A Commentary on the Mahayana Teaching of the Seven Points of Mind Training*. Boston and London: Shambhala Publications, 1987. A traditional presentation of lojong training.

Nalanda Translation Committee. *The Seven Points of Training the Mind*. Halifax, NS: Nalanda Translation Committee, 1993. A translation of the fifty-nine lojong slogans, printed on cards.

Namgyal, Zhechen Gyaltsab Padma Gyurmed. *Path of Heroes: Birth of Enlightenment*. Oakland, CA: Dharma Publishing, 1995. A traditional presentation of lojong training, including a modern commentary by Tarthang Tulku.

Rabten, Geshe, and Dhargyey, Geshe. *Advice from a Spiritual Friend*. London: Wisdom Publications, 1986. A traditional presentation of lojong training.

Shantideva. *The Way of the Bodhisattva*. Boston and London: Shambhala Publications, 1997. A classic text on the bodhisattva path of awakening. Chapter Three contains the bodhisattva's vow. Chapter Eight contains the contemplative practice of exchanging oneself for others.

Sogyal Rinpoche. *The Tibetan Book of Living and Dying*. San Francisco: Harper San Francisco, 1993. Chapter Twelve presents compassion practices, including tonglen.

Trungpa, Chögyam. *Glimpses of Mahayana*. Halifax, N.S.: Vajradhatu Publications (publication scheduled for Summer 2001). A brief, but excellent, introduction to the bodhisattva's path of compassion.

Trungpa, Chögyam. *Cutting Through Spiritual Materialism*. Berkeley: Shambhala Publications, 1973. See pp. 167–84 for a discussion of the bodhisattva's path.

Trungpa, Chögyam. *Meditation in Action*. Boulder: Shambhala Publications, 1969. See pp. 35–74 for a discussion of the six paramitas.

Trungpa, Chögyam. *The Myth of Freedom*. Berkeley and London: Shambhala Publications, 1976. See pp. 103–24 for a discussion of the bodhisattva's path.

Trungpa, Chögyam. *Shambhala: The Sacred Path of the Warrior*. Boston and London: Shambhala Publications, 1984. Teachings on the path of developing confidence and fearlessness in order to help others.

Trungpa, Chögyam. *Training the Mind and Cultivating Loving-Kindness*. Boston and London: Shambhala Publications, 1993. A contemporary presentation of lojong training. Tonglen is discussed on pp. 46–64.

Wallace, Alan B. *A Passage from Solitude: Training the Mind in a Life Embracing the World*. Ithaca, NY: Snow Lion Publications, 1992. A contemporary presentation of lojong training.

Wilber, Ken. *Grace and Grit*. Boston and London: Shambhala Publications, 1993.

For information regarding meditation instruction or inquiries about a practice center near you, please contact one of the following:

Shambhala International
1084 Tower Road
Halifax, Nova Scotia
Canada B3H 2Y5
Phone: (902) 425-4275 x 10   Fax: (902) 423-2750
Web: www.shambhala.org
This web site contains information about more than 100 Shambhala Centers.

Shambhala Europe
Annostrasse 20-27
D – 50678 Köln, Germany
Phone: 49 (0) 221 310 2400   Fax: 49 (0) 221 310 2450
Email: office@shambhala-europe.org

Karmê Chöling
369 Patneaude Lane
Barnet, Vermont 05821
Phone: (802) 633-2384   Fax: (802) 633-3012
Email: karmecholing@shambhala.org
Web: www.kcl.shambhala.org

Shambhala Mountain Center
4921 Country Road 68C
Red Feather Lakes, Colorado 80545
Phone: (970) 881-2184   Fax: (970) 881-2909
Email: rmsc@shambhala.org
Web: www.rmsc.shambhala.org

Gampo Abbey
Pleasant Bay, Nova Scotia
Canada B0E 2P0
Phone: (902) 224-2752   Fax: (902) 224-1521
Email: office@gampoabbey.org
Web: www.gampoabbey.org

Naropa University (formerly The Naropa Institute),
founded in 1974, is the only accredited, Buddhist-
inspired university in North America. For more information, contact:

Naropa University
2130 Arapahoe Avenue
Boulder, Colorado 80302
Phone: (303) 444-0202   Fax: (303) 444-0410
Email: info@naropa.edu
Web: www.naropa.edu

Audio- and videotape recordings of talks and seminars by Pema Chödrön are available from:

Great Path Tapes and Books
330 E. Van Hoesen Blvd.
Portage, Michigan 49002
Phone: (616) 384-4167   Fax: (425) 940-8456
Email: gptapes@aol.com
Web: www.pemachodrontapes.org

Kalapa Recordings
1084 Tower Road
Halifax, Nova Scotia
Canada B3H 2Y5
Phone: (902) 421-1550   Fax: (902) 422-3637
Web: www.shambhalamedia.org

Sounds True
413 S. Arthur Avenue
Louisville, Colorado 80027
Phone: 1-800-333-9185
Web: www.soundstrue.com